THE JUST INTONATION PRIMER

An Introduction to the Theory and Practice of Just Intonation

by David B. Doty

Third Edtion, December 2002

ISBN 0-9726810-0-0

©1993, 1994, 2002: David B. Doty

www.dbdoty.com/Words/Primer1.html
primer@dbdoty.com

Contents

- Preface to the Third Edition (2002) iv
- Preface to the Second Edition (1994) iv

Introduction 1

- What is Just Intonation? 1
- A Little History 2
  - Antiquity 2
  - The Middle Ages and the Renaissance 2
  - The Common-Practice Period
    and the Rise of Temperament 3
  - The End of Common Practice 5
- The Twentieth-Century Just Intonation Revival 6
- The Purpose of this Publication 7

Acoustic and Psychoacoustic Background 9

- Introduction 9
- Periodic Vibrations 9
- What is an Interval? 10
- Superposition of Pure Tones 11
  - Phase Relationships 12
  - Interference Beats 12
- The Harmonic Series 14
- Difference Tones 16
- Periodicity Pitch 17
- Complex Tones with Harmonic Partials 19
  - Coincident or Beating Harmonics 20
  - Arthur H. Benade's "Special Relationships" 22
  - Special Relationships Beyond the Octave .. 23
  - On the Consonance of Relationships
    Involving Higher Harmonics 24

Basic Definitions, Conventions, and Procedures 25

- Introduction 25
- Rules and Conventions 25
- Calculations with Ratios 25
  - Addition 25
  - Subtraction 25
  - Complementation 26
  - Converting Ratios to Cents 26
  - Dividing Just Intervals 26
  - Calculating Absolute Frequencies (Hz) 28
- The Harmonic Series and the Subharmonic Series 28
  - Converting Ratios to a Harmonic or
    Subharmonic Series Segment 28
  - Identities 30
- Prime Numbers, Primary Intervals,
  and Prime Limits 30
- What is a Chord? 30
- Interval Names 32
- Notation 32
- Anomalies 33
- Tetrachords and Tetrachordal Scales 33

The Ladder of Primes, Part One: Two, Three, and Five 35

- One, the Foundation 36
- Two, the Empty Matrix 36
- The Three Limit (Pythagorean Tuning) 36
  - The Pythagorean (Ditone) Diatonic Scale .. 36
  - Pythagorean Chromatic Scales
    and the Pythagorean Comma 37
  - Chords 38
- The Five Limit 38
  - Constructing a Five-Limit Major Scale 39
  - The Supertonic Problem 40
  - The Five-Limit Lattice 42
  - The Great Diesis 44
  - The Harmonic Duodene 45
  - Five Limit Chords 46
  - Condissonant Chords in the Five Limit 47
  - Deficiencies of the Five Limit 48

The Ladder of Primes, Part Two: Seven and Beyond 51

- Seven-Limit Intervals 51
  - New Consonances 51
  - Whole Tones 54
  - Semitones 54
  - Microtones 54
  - False Consonances 54
- Two Dimensional Planes in the
  Seven-Limit Fabric 55
- Seven Limit Chords 56
  - Subsets of the Dominant-Seventh
    and Ninth Chords 56
  - Diminished Triad 56

Half-Diminished Seventh Chord 57	Electronic Organs.. 70
"4-6-7" Chord 57	Stringed Instruments with
Seven-Limit Subharmonic Chords............. 57	One String per Note 70
Condissonant Chords in the Seven Limit ... 58	Fretted Instruments 71
Fixed Scales in the Seven Limit 59	Wind Instruments 73
The Higher Primes: Eleven, Thirteen,	Continuous-Pitch Instruments 74
and Beyond.. 59	"Natural Tendencies"................... 74
Eleven and Thirteen 59	Bowed Strings.............................. 75
Primary Intervals.. 61	Voices.. 76
Chords and Harmony 62	Trombones 76
Seventeen and Nineteen............................ 64	MIDI Synthesizers... 76
Beyond Nineteen... 65	Pitch Bend.................................... 76

PRACTICAL JUST INTONATION WITH REAL INSTRUMENTS 66

Introduction 66
Fixed-Pitch Instruments 67
    Acoustic Keyboards............................. 67
    Piano Problems 67
    Reed Organs 70
    Pipe Organs 70
    Electroacoustic Keyboards 70

Instruments with User-Programmable
Tuning Tables...................................... 77
Tuning Tables plus Pitch Bend 78
The MIDI Tuning-Dump Specification........ 78
Some Thoughts on Obtaining
Satisfactory Performances................................. 79

NOTES 81

INDEX 85

PREFACE TO THE THIRD EDITION (2002)

The third edition of *The Just Intonation Primer* contains no significant changes in content from the previous editions, though a few minor errors have been corrected. The type, however, has been completely reset and all of the art has been recreated from scratch. Why? The first and second editions of *The Primer* were produced with software that has long since become obsolete, necessitating the resetting of the type. As for the art, both my skills and the available tools have greatly improved since the production of the previous editions, and my standards, as well, have risen considerably.

This is not to say that I regard *The Primer*, as it now stands, as needing no improvement—quite the contrary. The problem is that once I began making improvements, there is no telling where the process would end. This would be contrary to my purpose for creating this third edition: to keep the publication available until I am able to complete the work that will supersede it. This is intended to be the last "print-only" edition of *The Just Intonation Primer*; any future editions will be in the form of multimedia products. There seems to be little purpose in merely *writing* about unfamiliar intervals, scales, and chords when it is now possible to present students with the actual sounds.

Thanks to Lucy A. Hudson for creating software that simplified the conversion of the text files from the previous edition.

PREFACE TO THE SECOND EDITION (1994)

The writing and initial publication of *The Just Intonation Primer* were made possible by a gift from a friend of the Just Intonation Network.

Thanks to Carola B. Anderson and Dudley Duncan for proofreading and commenting on *The Just Intonation Primer*. Thanks to Jim Horton for the use of his collection of obscure publications. Thanks to David Canright, John Chalmers, Merrill Gillespie, and La Monte Young for their suggestions of corrections to the first edition

INTRODUCTION

WHAT IS JUST INTONATION?

What is Just Intonation? Although, like most composers working with this unfamiliar tuning system, I am frequently asked this troublesome question, I have yet to devise an answer that is suitable for casual conversation. Technically, Just Intonation is any system of tuning in which all of the intervals can be represented by whole-number frequency ratios, *with a strongly implied preference for the simplest ratios compatible with a given musical purpose.* Unfortunately this definition, while concise and accurate, is more likely to result in a glazed expression indicative of confusion than in the gleam of understanding. It is, in short, a definition that is perfectly clear to the comparative few who have the background to understand it and who could, therefore, formulate it for themselves, and perfectly opaque to everyone else, including, unfortunately, most trained musicians. (It is my experience that most musicians are as ignorant of the details of twelve-tone equal temperament, the predominant tuning system in Western cultures for the past two hundred years, as they are of Just Intonation. If you doubt this, ask the next dozen musicians you meet to explain why there are twelve semitones in a chromatic scale and how to accurately tune those twelve equal semitones.) A detailed answer that incorporates all the necessary background on the physics of sound, the physiology and psychology of human hearing, the history of music, and the mathematics of tuning systems, far exceeds the limits of casual conversation. It could, in fact, fill a book.

A formal definition of Just Intonation may be difficult for the novice to grasp, but the aesthetic experience of just intervals is unmistakable. Although it is difficult to describe the special qualities of just intervals to those who have never heard them, words such as clarity, purity, smoothness, and stability come readily to mind. The supposedly consonant intervals and chords of equal temperament, which deviate from simple ratios to varying degrees, sound rough, restless, or muddy in comparison.

The simple-ratio intervals upon which Just Intonation is based are "special relationships" that the human auditory system is able to detect and distinguish from one another and from a host of more complex stimuli. They are what the human auditory system recognizes as consonance, if it ever has the opportunity to hear them in a musical context. Although the importance of these whole-number ratios is recognized both by musical tradition and by modern acoustic and psychoacoustic research, for the last two hundred years Western music has been burdened with a tuning system in which all of the supposed consonances, with the exception of the octave, deviate significantly from their optimal, integer-ratio forms. Indeed, some consonant intervals are so compromised in twelve-tone equal temperament that they are hardly represented at all.

Just Intonation provides a greater variety and superior quality of consonances and concords than equal temperament, but its resources are by no means limited to unrelieved consonance. Just Intonation also has the potential to provide more varied and powerful dissonances than the current system. This is the case in part because the simple, consonant intervals can be compounded in a great many ways to yield more complex dissonant intervals and, in part, because, the consonant intervals being truly consonant, the dissonances are rendered that much sharper in contrast. Further, because dissonances in Just Intonation are the products of concatenations of simpler intervals, consonance and dissonance coexist in a rational framework and their mutual relations are readily comprehensible.

The virtues of Just Intonation and the shortcomings of equal temperament are not limited to the affective properties of their respective intervals and chords. An equally serious problem with twelve-tone equal temperament is that it supplies composers with an artificially simplified, one-dimensional model of musical relationships. By substituting twelve equally spaced fixed tones for a potentially unlimited number of tones, interconnected by a web of subtle and complex musical relationships, equal temperament not only impoverished the sonic palette of Western music, but also deprived composers and theorists of the means for thinking clearly about tonal relationships, causing them to confuse close relationships with remote ones and consonances with dissonances. Not only does Just Intonation provide a vast array of superior new musical resources, but, when properly understood, provides the tools necessary for organizing and manipulating these greatly expanded resources.

Just Intonation is not a particular scale, nor is it tied to any particular musical style. It is, rather, a set of principles which can be applied to a limited number of musically significant intervals to generate an enormous variety of scales and chords, or to organize music without reference to any fixed scale. The principles of Just Intonation are applicable to any style of tonal or modal music (or even, if you wish, to atonal styles). Just Intonation is not primarily a tool for improving the consonance of existing musics, although it can, in some cases, be used this way. Just Intonation can give rise to new styles and forms of music which, although truly innovative, are, unlike those created by the proponents of the various "avant-garde-isms" of the twentieth century, comprehensible to the ear of the listener as well as to the intellects of the composer and analyst. Ultimately, Just Intonation is a method for understanding and navigating through the boundless reaches of the pitch continuum—a method that transcends the musical practices of any particular culture.

Just Intonation has depth and breadth. Its fundamental principles are relatively simple but its ramifications are vast. At present, the musical realm that comprises Just Intonation remains largely unexplored. A few pioneering composers and theorists have sketched some of its most striking features, but the map still contains many blank spaces where the adventurous composer may search for new musical treasures.

A Little History

In light of its numerous virtues, why isn't Just Intonation currently in general use? Like so many of our peculiar customs, this is largely an accident of history. A detailed history of tuning in the West would require a book of considerable length in its own right, and is thus far beyond the scope of the current work. No one has, as yet, written a comprehensive study of this subject. Until such becomes available, the reader is advised to consult Harry Partch's *Genesis of a Music*, especially Chapter Fifteen, "A Thumbnail Sketch of the History of Intonation,"[1] and J. Murray Barbour's *Tuning and Temperament*.[2] The following short sketch is intended only to describe, in general terms, how musical intonation in the West achieved its current, peculiar state.

Antiquity

Just Intonation is not a new phenomenon. The basic discovery that the most powerful musical intervals are associated with ratios of whole numbers is lost in antiquity.[3,4] Perhaps it was first discovered by the priestly musicians of Egypt or Mesopotamia in the second or third millennium B.C.E. Some scholars, most notably Ernest G. McClain, regard this discovery as of vital importance to the development of mathematics and religion in these ancient societies. The semimythical Greek philosopher Pythagoras of Samos (c. 560–480 B.C.E.) is generally credited with introducing whole-number-ratio tunings for the octave, perfect fourth, and perfect fifth into Greek music theory in the sixth century B.C.E. In the generations following Pythagoras, many Greek thinkers devoted a portion of their energies to musical studies and especially to scale construction and tuning. These musical philosophers, known collectively as the *harmonists*, created a host of different tunings of the various Greek scales, which they expressed in the form of whole-number ratios. The discoveries of the Greek harmonists constitute one of the richest sources of tuning lore in the world and continue to this day to exercise a significant influence on Western musical thought. Although most of the original writings of the harmonists have been lost, much of their work was summarized by the second century C.E. Alexandrian, Claudius Ptolemy, in his *Harmonics*. Ptolemy made significant contributions in his own right to the field of music theory, as well as to astronomy and geography.

The Middle Ages and the Renaissance

Since the time of the Greek harmonists, the idea of simple ratios as the determinants of musical consonance has never been wholly absent from Western musical thought. Although much Greek music theory was lost to the West with the fall of the Roman Empire, some was retained and passed on to medieval Europe, primarily through the musical writings of the late Roman philosopher Anicius Manlius Severinus Boethius (c. 480–525/6 C.E.). (Greek music theory was also preserved and further developed in the Islamic sphere, but this does not appear to have had much influence on musical developments in the West.) Throughout the Middle Ages, Western music was theoretically based on what is called Pythagorean intonation, a subset of Just Intonation based on ratios composed only of multiples of 2 and 3, which will be described in detail in Chapter Three. Pythagorean tuning is characterized by consonant octaves, perfect fourths, and perfect fifths, based on ratios of the numbers 1, 2, 3, and 4. All other intervals in Pythagorean tuning are dissonant. This property is consistent with the musical practice of the middle ages, in which polyphony was based on fourths, fifths, and octaves, with all other intervals, including thirds and sixths, being treated as dissonances.

In the later Middle Ages and early Renaissance, thirds and sixths were increasingly admitted into polyphonic music as consonances, and music theory was gradually modified to account for the existence of these consonant intervals, although it appears to have lagged considerably behind musical practice. Eventually, theorists were forced to partially abandon the Pythagorean framework of the middle ages in order to explain the existence of consonant thirds and sixths, because the most consonant possible thirds and sixths are based on ratios involving 5. The association of consonant thirds and sixths with ratios involving 5 was first mentioned by the English monk Walter Odington (c. 1300), but it took a long time for this idea to penetrate the mainstream of musical thought and displace the Pythagorean intonational doctrines—indeed, it can be argued that it never wholly succeeded in doing so. In the sixteenth century, the rediscovery of Greek writings on music, especially the writings of Ptolemy, gave considerable added ammunition to the advocates of consonant thirds and sixths based on ratios involving 5. In general, music theorists of the Italian Renaissance came to agree with the proposition of the Venetian Gioseffe Zarlino (1517–1590) that consonance was the product of ratios of the integers 1–6 (the so-called *senario*). The ratios that define the major and minor triads were discovered in the senario and were acclaimed as the most perfect concords, thereby setting the stage for the development of chordal, harmonic music in the subsequent "common practice" period.

The Common-Practice Period and the Rise of Temperament

Alas, while Renaissance theorists considered just intervals the foundation of melody and harmony, there was also a fly in the proverbial ointment, in the form of the growth of independent instrumental music featuring fixed-pitch fretted and keyboard instruments. The polyphonic music of the Middle Ages and the Renaissance was predominantly vocal music and the human voice, when properly trained and coupled to a sensitive ear, is readily capable of the subtle intonational adjustments required to perform sophisticated music in Just Intonation. The same can hardly be said for fretted strings or keyboard instruments. A player of a lute, guitar, or viol can make some expressive adjustment of pitch, it is true, but certainly has not the same degree of flexibility as a singer.[5] An organ or harpsichord can produce only those tones that its pipes or strings have been tuned to. For reasons that will not be explained here, but which will be made plain in subsequent chapters, a fixed-pitch instrument intended to play in perfect Just Intonation in more than a few closely related keys requires far more than twelve tones per octave, an arrangement that had already become standard by the fifteenth century. In fact, some experimental keyboard instruments with far more than twelve keys per octave were built during the sixteenth and seventeenth centuries but, presumably because of their added cost and complexity, these instruments did not become popular and the mainstream of musical thought and activity adopted a different solution to the problem of intonation on fretted strings and keyboard instruments: that of *temperament*.

The basic premise of temperament is that the number of pitches required to play in different keys can be reduced by compromising the tuning of certain tones so that they can perform different functions in different keys, whereas in Just Intonation a slightly different pitch would be required to perform each function. In other words, temperament compromises the quality of intervals and chords in the interest of simplifying instrument design and construction and playing technique. Many different schemes of temperament were proposed in the Renaissance and baroque eras, but, at least where keyboard instruments were concerned, they eventually coalesced into a type of tuning known as *meantone temperament*. (According to many writers, equal temperament was always the preferred system for lutes and viols, because it greatly simplified the placement and spacing of the frets.) Meantone temperament aims to achieve perfect major thirds and acceptable major and minor triads in a group of central keys, at the expense of slightly flatted fifths in those same central keys and some bad thirds and triads and one very bad fifth in more remote keys. The exemplary variety of meantone temperament, called quarter-comma meantone, produced, in a twelve-tone realization, eight good major triads and eight good minor triads, with the remaining four triads of each type being badly mistuned.[6] Meantone tunings satisfied the needs of composers for a time, but as instrumental music became more complex and the desire to modulate to more remote keys increased, the bad triads became a barrier to progress. As a result, musicians gradually adopted another system, twelve-tone equal temperament.

There is some uncertainty as to who deserves the credit or blame for the invention of equal temperament. It seems to have been the product of many minds working along convergent lines over a number of decades, if not centuries.[7] The French monk and mathematician Marin Mersenne (1588–1648) gave an accurate description of equal temperament and instructions for tuning it on a variety of instruments in his most important work, the *Harmonie Universelle* (1639), thereby contributing substantially to its popularization, but the practical adoption of equal temperament, like its invention, was a gradual process, occurring at different rates in different countries. Equal temperament seems to have first found favor for keyboard instruments in Germany, where some organs were so tuned as early as the last quarter of the seventeenth century, although it was still a subject of debate there seventy-five years later. Meantone seems still to have been the predominant system in France in the mid-eighteenth century, and in England meantone continued to be the predominant tuning, at least for organs, until the middle of the nineteenth century. The commonly held assumption that J.S. Bach was an advocate of equal temperament and that he wrote the twenty-four preludes and fugues of *The Well-Tempered Clavier* to demonstrate its virtues is at least debatable. The term "well temperament" was used in the eighteenth century to describe a species of temperament in which all keys were usable and in which the principal consonances of the most central keys often retained their just forms. In well temperaments, different keys had different characters, depending on their closeness to or remoteness from the key on which the tuning was centered. This latter characteristic was considered desirable by many baroque composers and theorists, who believed that different keys had characteristic colors and emotional effects.

Twelve-tone equal temperament, unlike meantone, mistunes all consonant intervals except the octave. Also unlike meantone, twelve-tone equal temperament favors perfect fifths over thirds. The equally tempered perfect fifth is approximately two cents narrower than the just perfect fifth (one cent = $^1/_{100}$ tempered semitone or $^1/_{1200}$ octave), whereas the equally tempered major third is approximately fourteen cents wider than the just major third, and the equally tempered minor third is approximately sixteen cents narrower than the just minor third. In a sense, the rise of equal temperament can be seen as a partial resurgence of the old Pythagorean doctrine, since the Pythagorean tuning also produced good perfect fifths (and fourths), wide major thirds, and narrow minor thirds. The major advantage of equal temperament over meantone is that every key in equal temperament is equally good (or equally bad). There is no contrast in consonance between keys, so all twelve tones can serve equally well as keynotes of major or minor scales or as the roots of major or minor triads.

Equal temperament was not adopted because it sounded better (it didn't then and it still doesn't, despite two hundred years of cultural conditioning) or because composers and theorists were unaware of the possibility of Just Intonation. The adoption of twelve-tone equal temperament was strictly a matter of expediency. Equal temperament allowed composers to explore increasingly complex chromatic harmonies and remote modulations without increasing the complexity of instrument design or the difficulty of playing techniques. These benefits, as we shall see, were not without costs.

Throughout the baroque and classical eras, while music, at least on keyboard instruments, was dominated first by meantone temperament, then by equal temperament, theorists continued to explain musical consonance as the product of simple, whole-number ratios. Considerable advances were made in the scientific understanding of sound production by musical instruments and of the human auditory mechanism during this period. Ironically, Mersenne, who played such a significant role in the popularization of twelve-tone equal temperament, also first detected and described the presence of the harmonic series in the composite tone of a vibrating string and in the natural tones of the trumpet. Mersenne was also the first theorist to attribute consonance to ratios involving 7, the next step up the harmonic series from Zarlino's senario. Later theorists, most notably Jean Philippe Rameau (1683–1784), appropriated the harmonic series as further support from "nature" for the primacy of whole-number ratios as the source of consonance. It apparently did not strike most of the theorists of the seventeenth and eighteenth centuries as problematic that, although they formed the theoretical basis for the whole of contemporary harmonic practice, simple-ratio intervals were gradually being purged from musical practice in favor of tempered approximations.

In the nineteenth century, a vigorous attack on equal temperament was mounted by Hermann von Helmholtz

(1821–1894), surgeon, physicist, and physiologist, and father of modern scientific acoustics and psychoacoustics. Helmholtz considerably advanced scientific understanding of the production and perception of musical sound, and proposed the first truly scientific theory of consonance and dissonance. He was a strong advocate of Just Intonation and deplored the effect that equal temperament had on musical practice, particularly with regard to singing. Contemporary with Helmholtz's studies there was a good deal of interest in the invention of experimental keyboards for Just Intonation (primarily organs or harmoniums), particularly in Great Britain. Among those engaged in this activity, the most notable were General Perronet Thompson, Colin Brown, and R.H.M. Bosanquet. Unfortunately, the proposals of Helmholtz and the other intonational reformers of the nineteenth century appear to have had no detectable effect on contemporary musical practice, although Helmholtz's work, in particular, was to have a significant influence on musicians of subsequent generations. Nineteenth century composers were still enamored of the facility for modulation and for the building of increasingly complex harmonies that equal temperament provided, and it was not until these resources were exhausted that any alternative was seriously considered.

THE END OF COMMON PRACTICE
Initially, the effect of equal temperament on Western music was probably beneficial. Composers obtained the ability to modulate freely and to build complex chromatic harmonies that had been impossible under the meantone system. As a result, abstract instrumental music flourished as never before, yielding what is generally considered the "golden age" of Western music. Like a plant stimulated by chemical fertilizers and growth hormones, music based on equal temperament grew rapidly and luxuriously for a short period—then collapsed. If equal temperament played a prominent role in stimulating the growth of harmonic music in the common-practice era, it played an equally large part in its rapid demise as a vital compositional style. Twelve-tone equal temperament is a limited and closed system. Once you have modulated around the so-called circle of fifths, through its twelve major and twelve minor keys, and once you have stacked up every combination of tones that can reasonably be considered a chord, there is nowhere left to go in search of new resources.

This is essentially where Western composers found themselves at the beginning of the twentieth century. Everything that could be done with the equally tempered scale and the principles of tonal harmony had been tried, and the system was breaking down. This situation led many composers to the erroneous conclusion that consonance, tonality, and even pitch had been exhausted as organizing principles. What was really exhausted was merely the very limited resources of the tempered scale. By substituting twelve equally spaced tones for a vast universe of subtle intervallic relationships, the composers and theorists of the eighteenth and nineteenth centuries effectively painted Western music into a corner from which it has not, as yet, extricated itself. Twentieth century composers have tried in vain to invent or discover new organizing principles as powerful as the common-practice tonal system. Instead, they have created a variety of essentially arbitrary systems, which, although they may seem reasonable in the minds of their creators, fail to take into account the capabilities and limitations of the human auditory system. These systems have resulted in music that the great majority of the population find incomprehensible and unlistenable.

Given that equal temperament had only been in general use for about 150 years at the time, it may seem strange that so few of the composers of the early twentieth century recognized that the cure for music's ills lay, at least in part, in the replacement of its inadequate tuning system. (Some theorists and composers did, in fact, advocate the adoption of new, microtonal tuning systems, but most of these proposals were for microtonal equal temperaments, such as quarter tones, third tones, sixth tones, eighth tones, or the like, which merely divided the existing twelve-tone scale into smaller, arbitrary intervals, and which made no improvement in the tuning of Western music's most fundamental intervals.) However, despite its fairly recent origin, equal temperament had already become quite deeply entrenched in Western musical thought and practice. There were several reasons for this. One was the industrial revolution. The nineteenth century saw the redesign and standardization of many instruments, particularly the orchestral woodwinds and brass. Strictly speaking, only fixed-pitch instruments (the piano, organ, harp, tuned percussion, and fretted strings) require temperament, the others being sufficiently flexible as to adjust pitch as musical context requires. Nevertheless, brass and woodwind instruments were also standardized to play a chromatic scale such that the "centers" of their pitches corresponded as closely as possible to the pitches of twelve-tone equal temperament. Another reason for the persistence of equal temperament was the repertory of the common-practice period. The previous 150 years had witnessed the development of the orchestra as we know it, along with its repertory, and the concert system that supported it. It had also seen the evolution of the piano, the preeminent equally tempered instrument, as the predominant instrument for both solo performance and accompaniment, and as the most important tool in musical education. The orchestra, the piano, and their players, trained to perform the works of eighteenth and nineteenth century composers, were the resources that turn-of-the-twentieth-century composers had to use if they wished to have their music performed. And all of these resources were dedicated to music that assumed equal temperament. It was little wonder, then, that few composers were willing to challenge this massive establishment in order to work in some new, untested tuning system.

The Twentieth-Century Just Intonation Revival

Although most composers were sufficiently intimidated by the weight of eighteenth and nineteenth century musical practice, fortunately a few were not. The first twentieth century composer to make a serious commitment to Just Intonation and the person primarily responsible for the revival of Just Intonation as a viable musical resource was Harry Partch (1901–1974), the iconoclastic American composer, theorist, instrument builder, dramatist, and musical polemicist. When Partch began his compositional career, no one, to the best of my knowledge, was making music in Just Intonation. Beginning with tentative experiments in the mid-1920s and continuing over a span of fifty years, Partch developed a system of Just Intonation with forty-three tones to the octave, built a large ensemble of predominantly stringed and percussion instruments to play in this tuning system, composed and staged six major musical theater pieces, along with numerous lesser works, and produced and distributed his own records. In 1949, Partch published the first edition of his *Genesis of a Music*, an account of his musical theories, instruments, and compositions that became the bible for subsequent generations of Just Intonation composers.

Whereas in previous centuries the goal of most intonational theorists was to find the ideal or most practical tuning for a culturally predominant scale, such as a major, minor, or chromatic scale, the approach of twentieth century composers and theorists working with Just Intonation, as exemplified by Partch, has been quite different. The goal of these artists has been, in most cases, to discover or create tunings that best served their own particular musical goals, whether for a single composition or for a lifetime's work, rather than one that could serve the needs of the culture as a whole.

From when he began work in the mid-1920s until the mid-1950s, Partch was the only composer in the United States doing significant work in Just Intonation. In the 1950s, Partch was joined by Lou Harrison (1917–2003) and Ben Johnston (b. 1926). Harrison first learned about Just Intonation from Partch's *Genesis of a Music*. He composed his first major work in Just Intonation, *Four Strict Songs for Eight Baritones and Orchestra*, in 1954.[8] Although, unlike Partch, he does not work exclusively in Just Intonation, Harrison has written a large body of work in various just tunings. He is probably best known for the creation, in conjunction with his companion, William Colvig, of a number of justly tuned American gamelan (Indonesian-style tuned percussion ensembles) and for the body of music he has composed for this medium, but he has also composed just music for a great variety of instrumental and vocal ensembles, often mixing elements from European and Asian musical traditions. Through his teaching at San Jose State University and Mills College in California and his extensive lecturing, he has introduced many younger composers to Just Intonation.

Ben Johnston discovered the possibility of Just Intonation early in life, when he attended a lecture on Helmholtz at age eleven. Later, he, like Harrison, discovered Partch's *Genesis of a Music*. Johnston contacted Partch and for a six month period in 1950 was his student and apprentice in the remote California coastal town of Gualala. Johnston began composing seriously in Just Intonation in 1959. Unlike Partch and Harrison, Johnston's work in Just Intonation employs mainly Western musical forms and instrumental combinations. His earlier work, through the early 1970s, generally combines extended microtonal Just Intonation with serial techniques. His later work tends to be simpler and more tonal, but still uses serialism at least occasionally. Johnston's works include eight string quartets in Just Intonation and numerous vocal and chamber ensemble pieces. He is also the inventor of a system of notation for extended Just Intonation that is used in this primer.

In the 1960s and 1970s, interest in Just Intonation continued to slowly increase. La Monte Young (b. 1935) began working with Just Intonation in the early 1960s in the context of his instrumental/vocal performance group, *The Theater of Eternal Music*. In this ensemble, Young developed the practice of performing long, static compositions based on selected tones from the harmonic series, played on various combinations of amplified instruments and voices. In 1964, Young began work on his semi-improvisational, justly tuned piano composition, *The Well-Tuned Piano*, which can be from five to seven hours in duration and which continues to evolve at the time of this writing. Young is also known for *The Dream House*, a living environment in which a number of electronically generated, harmonically related tones are sustained over a period of months or years.

Terry Riley (b. 1935), who was a member of Young's *Theater of Eternal Music* at various times in the early 1960s, is known primarily as a keyboard composer/improviser. He is perhaps best known as the composer of the early minimalist piece *In C* (1964), which is not explicitly a Just Intonation piece, although it has sometimes been performed this way. In the 1970s, Riley performed extensively on a modified electronic organ tuned in Just Intonation and accompanied by tape delays. More recently, he has been performing his work on justly tuned piano and digital synthesizers, and composing for other ensembles, especially the string quartet.

In the late 1970s and early 1980s the number of composers working with Just Intonation began to increase significantly, due in part to the development of affordable electronic instruments with programmable tuning capabilities and in part to the coming of age of the post–World War II generation of composers. The achievements of Partch, Harrison, Johnston, Young, and Riley made it evident to these younger composers that Just Intonation was a valuable resource for composers of diverse styles and tastes, and the availability of electronic instruments with programmable tuning made it possible for the first time for composers to experiment with a variety of different tuning systems without having to invent and build novel instruments or to train performers in unusual playing techniques. Changing the pitches available on a digital synthesizer simply means changing the data values in a tuning table or switching to a different table. If the instrument and its operating software have been designed to facilitate such changes, either of these functions can be performed virtually instantaneously by a computer running appropriate software. Hence, a conventional keyboard can be used to play a virtually unlimited number of different pitches. This capability has, for all intents and purposes, eliminated the condition that first brought temperament into being: the necessity of restricting the number of pitches used in music to the number of keys available on an affordable, playable keyboard.

Among the many composers currently doing significant work in Just Intonation are William C. Alves, Lydia Ayers, Jon Catler, David Canright, Dean Drummond, Cris Forster, Glenn Frantz, Ellen Fullman, Kraig Grady, Michael Harrison, Ralph David Hill, David Hykes, Douglas Leedy, Norbert Oldani, Larry Polansky, Robert Rich, Daniel Schmidt, Carter Scholz, James Tenney, and Erling Wold. The variety of musical styles represented by this group is extremely diverse, and the use of Just Intonation may be the only feature they all share. Although more than half work primarily or exclusively with electronic media, they also include exponents of Partch's tradition of acoustic instrument building (Drummond and Grady), Lou Harrison's American gamelan movement (Schmidt), Young's and Riley's improvisational keyboard styles (M. Harrison), a harmonic singer (Hykes), and even a justly tuned rock guitarist (Catler).

THE PURPOSE OF THIS PUBLICATION

Although the technical barriers to the composition and performance of significant music in Just Intonation have been considerably reduced in recent years, barriers of another type remain largely in place, namely the weight of custom and the lack of accessible information on principles of Just Intonation. The colleges, universities, and conservatories continue to teach a curriculum based on music of the common-practice era, in which alternate tunings are unlikely to receive more than a passing mention. With the exception of the fortunate few who find themselves in institutions with a microtonal composer or theorist on the faculty, students who develop an interest in these matters are unlikely to receive much support or encouragement, much less practical instruction, from the academic establishment. Such students, if they persist, generally find it necessary to educate themselves, and in the process often have to reinvent or rediscover principles and structures that are well known to more experienced composers.

In an attempt to remedy this situation, in the fall of 1984, I and my associates in the experimental music ensemble Other Music, in consultation with a number of other West Coast Just Intonation composers and theorists, founded the Just Intonation Network. The Just Intonation Network is a nonprofit group fostering communication among composers, musicians, instrument designers, and theorists working with Just Intonation. Its primary goal is to make information about the theory and practice of composition in Just Intonation available to all who want or need it. The primary method for distributing this information is the network's journal, **1/1**, the only current periodical devoted primarily or exclusively to Just Intonation. For the past eighteen years I have served as editor of this publication.

A survey of Just Intonation Network members taken several years ago revealed that more than half were newcomers to the study of Just Intonation who found a significant portion of the articles in **1/1** over their heads. It was with the goal of assisting these readers that the *Just Intonation Primer* was conceived. The *Just Intonation Primer*, as its title indicates, is not intended to provide a complete or comprehensive course in the theory and practice of Just Intonation, let alone tuning in general or other aspects of composition. Its purpose, rather, is to provide the reader with the basic information and skills necessary to read and comprehend intermediate and advanced texts such as articles in **1/1** or Harry Partch's *Genesis of a Music*, and to prepare the reader to begin independent study and composition.

The *Primer* is intended for readers with at least an elementary knowledge of common-practice Western music theory, including the basic terminology of intervals, chords, and scales, and the fundamentals of harmony. The reader is not assumed to have any prior knowledge of Just Intonation or of alternative tunings in general, nor is the reader expected to be a mathematician or number theorist. The only math required to understand this book is basic arithmetic, in combination with some simple procedures explained in Chapter Three. An inexpensive scientific calculator will prove useful for comparing the sizes of intervals.

ACOUSTIC AND PSYCHOACOUSTIC BACKGROUND

INTRODUCTION

In this chapter we will examine some of the factors that make Just Intonation both possible and musically desirable. The principal determinants of the way we hear tones of definite pitch and, most importantly, relations among such tones, are to be found in the construction of the human auditory system: the ear and its associated neural circuitry. We will show that the human auditory system is specially equipped to recognize and distinguish among pitch relationships that can be represented by simple integer ratios. This fact is responsible for the selection of the particular musical intervals which form the foundation of music in the West and in many others of the world's more musically sophisticated cultures, and is also responsible for the selection of the relatively small variety of vibrating systems that characterize most of our musical instruments.

The physics of musical instruments, the physiology of the human auditory system, and the psychology of music are complex fields, in which many important questions remain to be answered. It is not possible, in the limited space available here, to explore these closely related topics in depth. We must limit ourselves to an examination of those factors that have a direct bearing on interval perception. In the discussion that follows, some simplification will be unavoidable. While all of the statements about musical vibrating systems and human hearing that follow are, as generalizations, accurate, these systems are complex, and upon closer examination will often present exceptions to rules derived from simplified models. The reader is strongly encouraged to study these subjects in greater depth. Every composer and musician, but especially those involved in exploring alternate tuning systems, should have a solid understanding of the physics of sound and the physiology of the human auditory system. Intellectually curious listeners, too, may find the study of these subjects rewarding.

PERIODIC VIBRATIONS

When we examine the properties of sound and of the human auditory system in search of the principles which govern tuning, we must focus our attention on the generation and perception of tones of definite pitch, since only these tones are subject to precise tuning. Tones of definite pitch are the products of periodic vibrations—motions that repeat in a consistent pattern at a consistent time interval. Such vibrations originate as periodic motions executed by the sounding elements of musical instruments or by the human vocal apparatus. These motions disturb the surrounding air, creating periodic variations in pressure. Because air is an elastic medium, these periodic pressure variations propagate or radiate outward from their sources as waves, like ripples in a pond. They continue to do so until they are reflected, absorbed, or dissipated by friction. When struck with sufficient force by such vibrations, our eardrums move in and out in a manner corresponding to the variations in pressure, setting up a chain of events in the middle and inner ear which ultimately results in the conversion of these mechanical vibrations into nerve impulses, which the brain interprets as sound.

Periodic vibrations are typically graphed in the manner shown in Figure 2.1 This type of graph represents changes in pressure observed at a particular location over a period of time. The vertical axis of the graph represents pressure variation relative to a state of equilibrium, which is labeled as zero. Values above zero represent increased air pressure (compression) and values below zero represent decreased air pressure (rarefaction). The horizontal axis represents the passage of time.

The vibration graphed in Figure 2.1 represents the simplest possible periodic vibration, which physicists refer to as "simple harmonic motion." This type of vibration is also known as a sine wave or sinusoid, because it corresponds to the graph of the trigonometric *sine* function. When simple harmonic motion is perceived

Figure 2.1. Graph of a simple periodic vibration

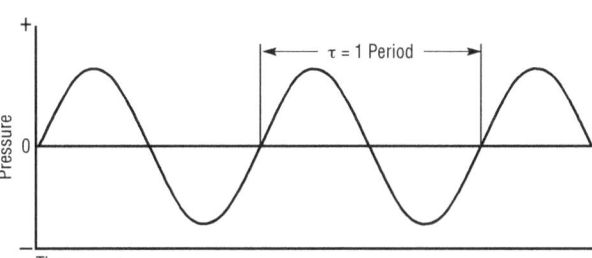

Figure 2.2: Two pure tones of differing amplitude

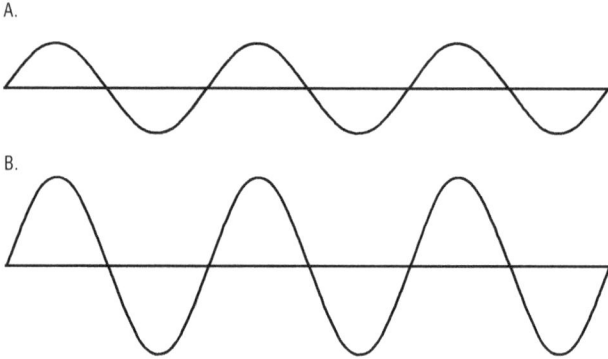

as sound, we refer to the result as a pure or simple tone. Except in certain electronic or computer-generated compositions, pure tones are rarely heard in music. A tuning fork struck gently, a flute played in its upper register without vibrato, or the phoneme "oo" sung in a falsetto voice all approximate a pure tone. While pure tones as such are rare in music, they are very important for the study of acoustics and psychoacoustics because it has been demonstrated that the more complex periodic vibrations produced by musical instruments and the human voice can be understood as the result of many pure tones of different frequencies sounding simultaneously.

Periodic vibrations possess a number of musically significant properties. From an intonational perspective, the most significant of these properties is the *frequency* of vibration, that is, the rate at which the periodic vibration recurs. In Figure 2.1, the Greek letter τ designates the time required for one complete cycle of vibration. We call the time required for one complete cycle the *period* of the wave. The frequency of the vibration is directly related to its period. It is defined by the number of periods or cycles that occur in one second. In mathematical terms, frequency = $1/\tau$. For example, if the time interval τ in Figure 2.1 represented 0.01 seconds, the frequency of the vibration would be 100 cycles per second. The frequencies of sounds and other periodic vibrations are normally expressed in Hertz (abbreviated Hz), where 1 Hz equals 1 cycle per second, so the proper notation for the above example would be 100 Hz.

The physical property of frequency corresponds in a predictable, measurable way to the musical/perceptual quality of pitch. Higher frequency vibrations are perceived as higher pitches and lower frequency vibrations are perceived as lower pitches. The human auditory mechanism recognizes as a sound of definite pitch any periodic vibration of sufficient energy which has a frequency in the range of 20 Hz–20,000 Hz. In musical terms, this is a range of somewhat less than ten octaves.[1] This range is approximate. There is significant variation among individuals, and the upper limit tends to decrease with increasing age and/or excessive exposure to loud sounds.

Two other musically significant properties of any periodic vibration are its amplitude and its waveform. Amplitude refers to the amount of variation in pressure that occurs within a cycle, corresponding to the height of the peaks and depth of the troughs in the graphic representation of the wave. The physical property of amplitude corresponds to the perceptual property of intensity or loudness. In Figure 2.2, the two waves have the same frequency and waveform, but wave B has twice the amplitude of wave A. Wave B is therefore the louder of the two sounds. It will not, however, be perceived as twice as loud as wave A. The relationship between change in amplitude and change in loudness is fairly complex, but since loudness has only a slight influence on intonation, we won't address that issue here.

A pure tone can vary in pitch (frequency) and in intensity (amplitude), but it cannot by definition vary in timbre. The musical property of timbre or tone color is associated with the waveform of a periodic vibration, that is, the shape of the pressure-variation curve for any given cycle.[2] A pure tone is always the product of a sine wave. Other, more complex periodic vibrations are the products of two or more pure tones (sine waves) sounding simultaneously at different frequencies. We will postpone an examination of waveform and timbre until we have examined the superposition of pure tones.

What is an Interval?

In considering issues involving tuning, we are concerned not with individual tones (periodic vibrations) but with relations between two or more tones. Music theory calls the relation between two tones of definite pitch an *interval*. In conventional Western music theory, intervals are named in accordance with the roles they play in diatonic scales. Names such as "major second," "minor third," "perfect fourth," "diminished fifth," and so forth evoke familiar experiences for Western-trained musicians (and, for this reason, we will sometimes make use of them), but they do not provide us with any information about the actual physical quantities (frequency relationships) involved. If we are to describe musical intervals with sufficient accuracy to allow tuning systems to be compared and analyzed, we must resort to numbers.

It is possible, of course, to describe any tuning in terms of the absolute frequencies of the tones involved. Tuning theory, however, is not primarily concerned with absolute frequency but with the precise relationships *between* frequencies. Consider the following two pairs of frequencies, expressed in Hz: (440, 660) and (528, 792). Although it is not apparent to the eye, both pairs of frequencies represent the same interval, a just perfect fifth. The first pair represents the tones A_4 and E_5, and the second pair represents C_5 and G_5 in a just tuning based on A = 440 Hz. What characteristic do these two pairs of frequencies have in common that would tip us off to the fact that they both represent the same interval? Perhaps it is the difference between the two frequencies. The difference between the first pair, 660 and 440, is 220 Hz. The difference between the second pair, 792 and 528, is 264 Hz. The latter quantity is twenty percent larger than the former, so it doesn't appear that the difference in Hz is the characteristic we are looking for. Obviously, neither the sum or the product of these two pairs of frequencies will be the same, either, so these can't be the clues we are seeking. The only other arithmetical operation that remains to be tried is division. In this case, we see that both $^{660}/_{440}$ and $^{792}/_{528}$ yield the same quotient, 1.5. Expressed differently, $^{660}/_{440}$ and $^{792}/_{528}$ are both equivalent to the simple ratio $^3/_2$. So are the pairs $^{2376}/_{1584}$, $^{1336.5}/_{891}$, $^{132}/_{88}$, and an infinite number of others that produce the musical sensation we recognize as a perfect fifth. Similarly, every other recognizable musical interval corresponds to a unique *frequency ratio*. The absolute frequencies that delineate an interval are not important, only their ratio. This is evident from the common practice of transposing musical compositions into different keys (that is, multiplying all of the frequencies by some constant factor). We hear the transposed composition as being higher or lower than the original version, but we recognize it as being the same composition because all of the frequency relationships (ratios) are preserved, although the frequencies themselves are altered. In contrast, if one were to shift the pitch of a musical composition by adding or subtracting a constant number of Hertz from the frequency of each tone, the result would be a bizarre distortion of the original, since all of the frequency ratios would be altered.

The intervals of Just Intonation, as stated in the introduction, are all expressible as ratios of whole numbers,

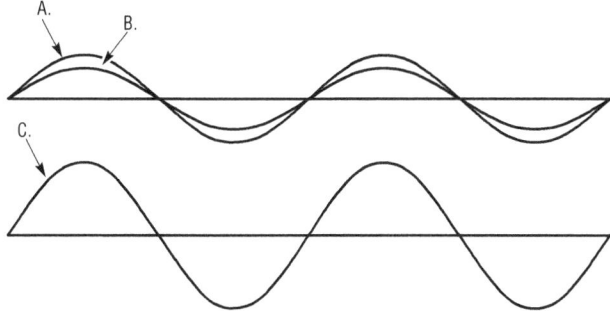

Figure 2.3: Superposition of two pure tones

with the most consonant intervals requiring the smallest numbers. With the exception of the octave, which has the ratio 2:1, none of the intervals of the twelve-tone equally tempered scale (or any other equal temperament) can be expressed as ratios of whole numbers. All of the intervals of twelve-tone equal temperament involve as a factor the twelfth root of two ($\sqrt[12]{2}$), an irrational number that is approximately 1.0594. Nevertheless, tempered intervals can be *approximated* by ratios; the perfect fifth of twelve-tone equal temperament, for example, is approximately 1.49827:1, a close approximation of the just 3:2 or 1.5. From the point of view of the Just Intonation enthusiasts, the ideal forms of musical intervals are those which can be expressed as ratios of whole numbers, whereas the intervals of other systems, which cannot be so represented, are only approximations of those ideals. Why this should be so is the subject of the remainder of this chapter.

SUPERPOSITION OF PURE TONES

Because pure tones are the basic building blocks of all periodic vibrations, there is much to be gained from examining how we hear pure tones. When two pure tones are sounded simultaneously, a number of phenomena of musical and acoustical interest can be observed. First, we will consider the case of two pure tones having exactly the same frequency. When two pure tones (or two tones of any sort whatever) sound simultaneously, their waveforms sum to produce a composite waveform. Figure 2.3 illustrates two such pure tones, represented by curves A and B, and the composite waveform, represented by curve C. This summation occurs because, at a given instant, a particular air molecule, or a particular point on your eardrum, can only be moving in one direction and at one specific velocity. That direction and velocity are the sum of however many different forces are acting on that point at the selected instant. In the case of Figure 2.3, the result is simply a pure tone with the same frequency as its two components and an amplitude that is the sum of their amplitudes.

Phase Relationships

Observe that the two pure tones in Figure 2.3 leave the equilibrium point at the same instant and remain exactly synchronized throughout their respective cycles. When two periodic vibrations are synchronized in this manner they are said to be *in phase*. Conversely, periodic vibrations that are not synchronized are said to be *out of phase*. Phase relations are expressed in degrees, with 360 degrees representing a full cycle. Figure 2.4 shows what happens when two pure tones of identical frequency and amplitude differ in phase by varying amounts. When the phase difference is 0 degrees or 360 degrees (A) the two components sum, as described above, to produce a composite wave that is in phase with both components. When the difference is 90 degrees (B) or 270 degrees (D) the composite waveform is still a pure tone of the same frequency as the two components, with an amplitude that is the sum of the amplitudes of the two components, and with a phase that is intermediate between that of the two components. Since the peaks and troughs of the two waves do not coincide, their combined amplitude is less than that in (A), where the two waves are in exact phase. (C) shows the two waves exactly 180 degrees or one-half cycle out of phase. In this case, the same rules apply, but since the peaks of one wave are exactly aligned with the troughs of the other and vice-versa, the sum of their amplitudes is zero, and no sound is heard. From these four examples we can easily envision what occurs with other phase relations. As the phase approaches 0 or 360 degrees, the combined amplitude of the waves approaches maximum, whereas when the phase approaches 180 degrees, the combined amplitude approaches its minimum. Remember we are only speaking of pure tones of identical frequency and amplitude. For waves of different forms, frequencies, or amplitudes, the situation will be more complex, but the composite wave will always be the sum of its components.

Interference Beats

Only vibrations with exactly the same frequency will remain in a constant phase relationship from cycle to cycle. When two tones of different frequencies are sounded together, their phase relationship will be in a

Figure 2.4: Pure tones in changing phase relationships

A. 0° Phase Difference

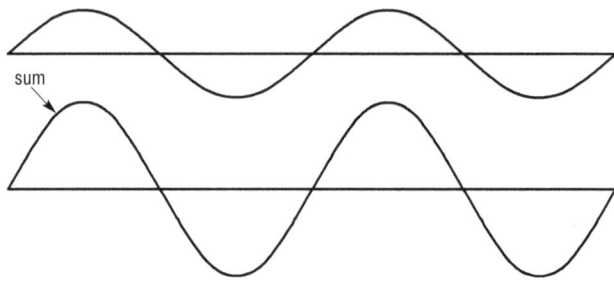

B. 90° Phase Difference

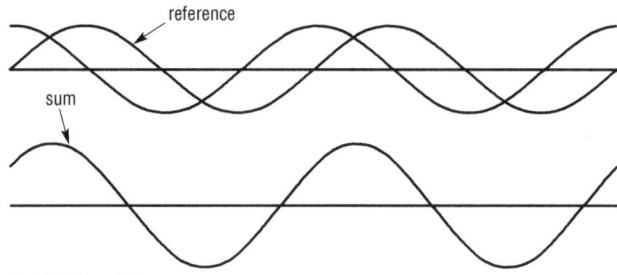

C. 180° Phase Difference

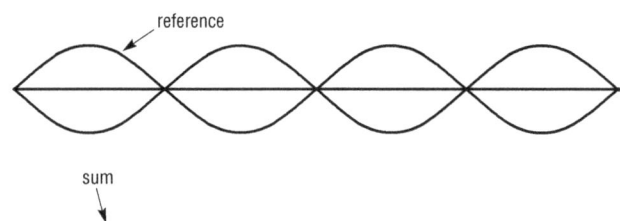

D. 270° Phase Difference

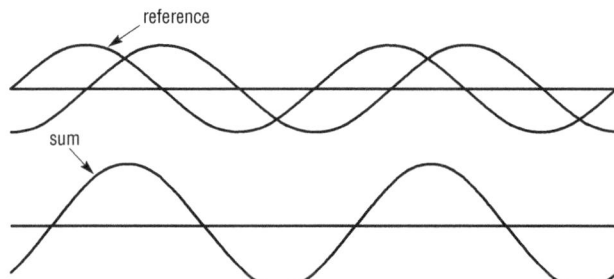

constant state of change. (Waves that are in an integer-ratio frequency relationship m:n, where *m* represents the higher frequency, will return to the same phase relationship after every *n* cycles of the lower frequency.) These facts have important consequences for the art of tuning. Figure 2.5 illustrates what happens when two pure tones with the same amplitude and slightly different frequencies are sounded together. At point A, the two tones are in phase and reinforce one another. At point B, the two

Figure 2.5: Interference beats of two pure tones

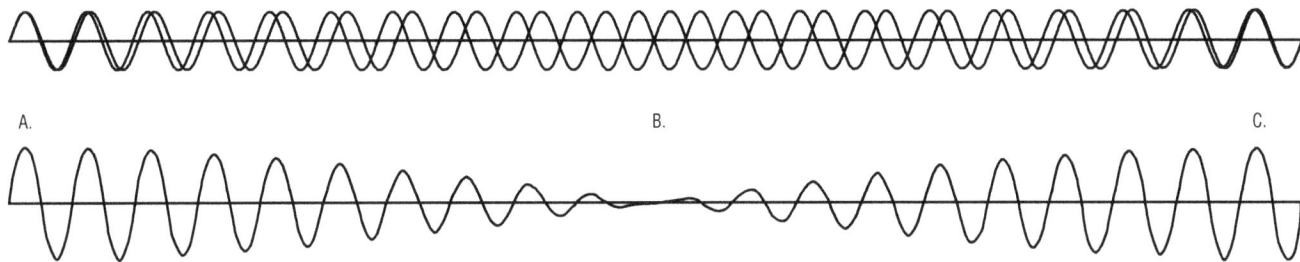

tones are 180 degrees out of phase, and therefore cancel one another. At point C, the two tones are back in their original relationship, and again reinforce one another. This pattern of alternate reinforcement and cancellation will continue at a constant rate as long as the two tones continue to sound at the specified frequencies. These periodic variations in amplitude are known as interference beats, or simply as beats. The beat frequency, f_B, is the difference between the two component frequencies ($f_2 - f_1$). It makes no difference which of the two tones is higher in frequency, the beat frequency will be the same in either case, occurring at the absolute value of the difference between the two frequencies. The amplitude variation is greatest when the two tones are of equal amplitude, as illustrated in the figure. This is the case because only two vibrations of exactly equal amplitude can cancel each other completely when they are out of phase by 180 degrees. When two pure tones of unequal amplitude are sounded together in the appropriate frequency relationship, beating takes the form of a periodic variation in amplitude, but complete cancellations do not occur. The greater the difference in the amplitudes of the two tones, the smaller the amplitude of the resulting beats.

When two pure tones give rise to interference beats as described above, the tones themselves are not heard as such. Rather, the listener hears a single, "fused" tone with a pitch that is the average of the two component frequencies and that varies in amplitude at the beat frequency. When the two tones move closer together in frequency, the beat frequency diminishes, the beats vanishing entirely when a perfect unison is achieved. When the two tones move apart in frequency, the beat frequency increases, until, at a rate of about 15 Hz – 20 Hz (the same threshold at which we begin to perceive tones of definite pitch), it becomes too fast for the ear to distinguish the individual beats. Beyond this threshold, we still hear a fused tone with a frequency that is the average of its two components, augmented by a characteristic "roughness" that is the product of rapid interference beats. As the two tones move farther apart, a point is eventually reached where the ear perceives two discrete tones. This point is known as the *limit of frequency discrimination*. Over most of the musical range, the limit of frequency discrimination for pure tones is in the vicinity of a whole tone. The roughness caused by rapid beating persists until the two tones are separated by a still larger interval, known as the *critical band*, which, over most of the musical range, falls between a minor third and a whole tone (Figure 2.6). The presence of interference beats or roughness is generally regarded as the principal cause of dissonance. In studies with pairs of pure tones, listeners generally identify maximum dissonance with intervals in the vicinity of twenty-five percent of the critical bandwidth. This varies from about three-fourths of a semitone in the lower part of the audio range to about one-half of a semitone in the upper part of the range.

Whereas the cause of interference beats should be obvious from the discussion above, the reason that the

Figure 2.6: The limit of frequency discrimination and the critical band

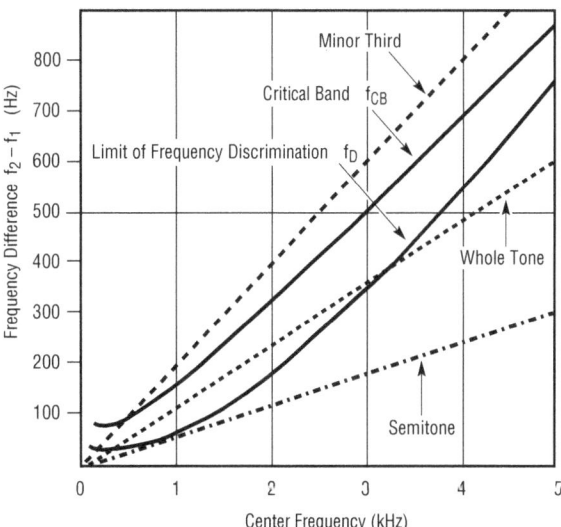

ACOUSTIC AND PSYCHOACOUSTIC BACKGROUND

Figure 2.7: A simplified representation of the cochlea

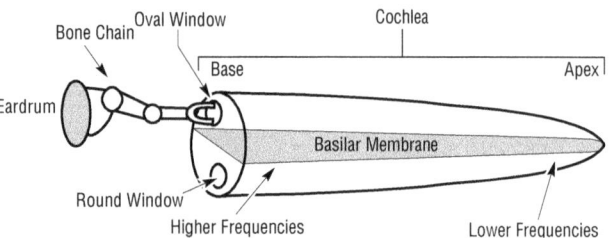

ear is unable to distinguish the individual tones that give rise to the beats requires further explanation. The explanation is to be found in the structure within the ear that is responsible for the conversion of sound waves into nerve impulses. Figure 2.7 is a schematic representation of middle and inner ear. The most important component of the inner ear is the cochlea. The cochlea is normally coiled like a snail shell, but in the illustration it has been straightened to reveal its internal structure. The cochlea is filled with an incompressible fluid called the perilymph, and is divided in two longitudinally by the basilar membrane. On the basilar membrane are located the hair cells that, when stimulated, generate the nerve impulses that the brain interprets as sound. When the eardrum is set in motion by vibrations in the air, these vibrations are transmitted from the eardrum to the cochlea by the chain of small bones in the middle ear. This chain of bones communicates with the cochlea by means of a membrane known as the oval window. Motion at the oval window sets up waves in the perilymph that correspond to the stimulus at the eardrum, and these waves, in turn, cause the basilar membrane to vibrate, in the manner of a flag flapping in the wind, stimulating the hair cells. Different frequencies cause different regions on the basilar membrane to vibrate. The areas sensitive to different frequencies are distributed along the membrane in order of frequency, with the lowest frequencies situated closest to the apex of the cochlea and the highest frequencies closest to the oval window. Thus, the spatial position on the basilar membrane of the hair cells which are stimulated by vibrations of a given frequency is thought to be the primary mechanism for frequency identification.

The resonance regions on the basilar membrane for different frequencies are not sharply defined. Rather, for any specific frequency there is an area of maximum resonance graduating into areas of diminishing resonance on either side. Hence, tones that are closer together in frequency than a certain limit have resonance regions that overlap. This overlap is believed to be the cause of fused tones and roughness. Tones that are so close together that their resonance regions on the basilar membrane overlap significantly cannot be individually discriminated, and are therefore perceived as a single, fused tone. The distance by which the resonance regions for two tones must be separated to avoid this fusion defines the limit of frequency discrimination. Tones which have resonance regions that are farther apart, but which still overlap somewhat, can be distinguished, but are accompanied by roughness. The distance by which the resonance regions for two tones must be separated to avoid any overlap defines the critical band.

THE HARMONIC SERIES

Figure 2.8 shows a portion of a pattern that is of paramount significance for the art and science of music. It is known as the harmonic series. The harmonic series is the series of all integer (positive whole-number) multiples of some frequency f ($f, 2f, 3f, 4f, 5f, \ldots$). Hence, the relationship between any two members of the series is an integer ratio. The figure illustrates the first sixteen members of the series on the pitch C_2, but what is significant is the pattern of intervals *between* the successive tones of the series, rather than the specific tones

Figure 2.8: The first sixteen harmonics of C_2

Figure 2.9: Summation of several harmonics

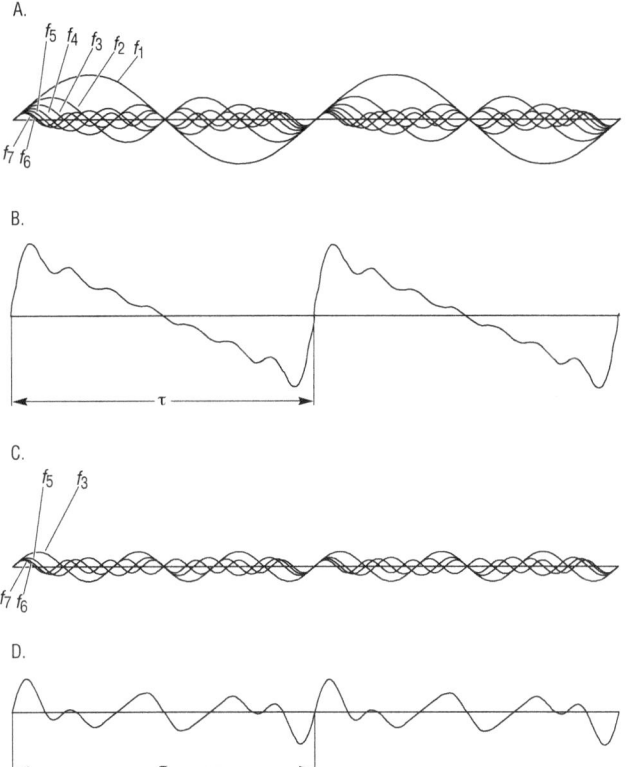

of the series. The series can be transposed to any starting frequency without altering its essential character. Although the series is represented here in a variant of conventional staff notation, all of the intervals of the series except the octave deviate significantly from those of the equally tempered scale (or to put things in a more proper order, the intervals of the tempered scale deviate from those of the harmonic series). The precise deviations, expressed in cents, where one cent = $1/100$ equal semitone or $1/1200$ octave, are given in column three of Table 2.1. (The method for calculating cents will be explained in a subsequent chapter, as will the meaning of the unusual accidentals used in the figure.)

When pure tones with relative frequencies that correspond to degrees of a harmonic series are superposed, the result is a complex waveform with a period and frequency that correspond to those of the first harmonic, which is also known as the *fundamental* of the series. This is the case even when neither the fundamental nor any of its octave multiples are present. The complex tones produced by the human voice and many (though not all) musical instruments are made up of many pure tones corresponding to degrees of a harmonic series.[3]

The simple components that make up a complex tone are known as its *partials*. When the relative frequencies of the partials of a complex tone correspond to the degrees of a harmonic series, they are said to be *harmonic partials* or simply *harmonics*. *Any complex periodic vibration can be analyzed as the sum of two or more harmonic partials*. When the relative frequencies of a set of partials deviate from the harmonic series, they are described as *inharmonic*. Complex vibrations that are *not* periodic are the products of inharmonic partials. The number of partials present in a given tone, their relative intensities, and the way their intensities vary over time are the primary determinants of the musical property known as timbre or tone color. The relative intensities of the different partials making up a given complex tone are referred to as the *harmonic spectrum* of that tone.

To prove that all complex periodic vibrations are the products of harmonic partials requires complex mathematics quite beyond the scope of this publication.[4] We can, however, provide a few concrete examples. Figure 2.9 (A) shows a group of seven pure tones with relative frequencies corresponding to the first seven degrees of a harmonic series. The relative amplitudes of the

Table 2.1: The first sixteen harmonics of C_2, with deviations from twelve-tone equal temperament

Harmonic Number	Nearest 12TET Pitch Name	Deviation from 12TET
1	C_2	0
2	C_3	0
3	G_3	+2
4	C_4	0
5	E_4	−14
6	G_4	+2
7	$B\flat_4$	−31
8	C_5	0
9	D_5	+4
10	E_5	−14
11	$F\sharp_5$	−49
12	G_5	+2
13	$A\flat_5$	+41
14	$B\flat_5$	−31
15	$B\natural_5$	−12
16	C_6	0

harmonics decrease in direct proportion to their ordinal numbers; that is, the second harmonic has one-half the amplitude of the first, the third harmonic has one-third the amplitude of the first, and so on. This is typical of the relative amplitudes of the harmonics of many common types of musical tones. (B) is the composite waveform resulting from the summation of the seven harmonics. (Electronic musicians will recognize this as an approximation of a sawtooth wave, a waveform easily generated with analog electronics and commonly used as raw material for subtractive synthesis.) Note that the period of the wave (τ), and hence its frequency, is equal to that of the fundamental. One could stack a great many more harmonic components on this wave, of any relative amplitudes and in any phase relation to the fundamental, and this fact would not change. As long as all of the components are integer multiples of the fundamental, the period and frequency of the composite wave will not change. (C) is the group of harmonics in (A) less the fundamental and its octave multiples (the first, second, and fourth harmonics). The composite waveform (D) is very different from waveform (B), and the resulting sound will be quite different in timbre, but the period and frequency are still the same as those of the missing fundamental.

When the human auditory system encounters a group of pure tones with relative frequencies that correspond to low-numbered degrees of a harmonic series sounding simultaneously, it does not normally hear several separate tones with distinct pitches.[5] Rather, it hears *a single entity*. This entity, as might be expected, is perceived as a tone with a pitch corresponding to the repetition rate of the composite wave, which, as we have seen, corresponds to that of the fundamental of the series. It is not necessary for the fundamental or one of its octave multiples to be among those tones actually being sounded for this response to occur, nor is it necessary for other conflicting tones to be absent. As few as two or three relatively low-numbered members of the series are sufficient to produce the sensation that the fundamental is being heard. Some of the reasons for this phenomenon will become clear in the discussion of simple tones and the human auditory system that follows.

One need not look far for the reason why our auditory system is specially equipped to recognize the harmonic series. All sustained, pitched sounds produced by the human voice consist of a portion of a harmonic series, with certain portions of the harmonic spectrum receiving a characteristic emphasis. The human auditory system is, of course, highly specialized for the recognition of human speech. We are all familiar with the so-called "cocktail-party effect," that is, the ability to pick out and understand a single human voice heard among a cacophony of other voices and miscellaneous noises. No doubt, our ability to discriminate sounds that possess harmonic components was developed to facilitate this kind of behavior (that is, understanding human speech amid a welter of conflicting sounds, not attending cocktail parties). This feature of the auditory system has had a tremendous effect on the shaping of music, both in terms of the selection of the vibrating bodies that are used in musical instruments and in the selection of the intervals that make up our chords and scales. In a very real sense, those sounds which match some portion of the harmonic series are signal and all the rest is noise.[6]

We will return to complex tones with harmonic partials later in this chapter, but first we will examine some additional phenomena associated with pure tones that contribute to the recognition of integer-ratio intervals as a special class of phenomena.

DIFFERENCE TONES

When two or more pure tones are sounded simultaneously with sufficient intensity, the nonlinear response of the ear may generate additional tones that are musically significant. These tones are known variously as combination tones, resultant tones, summation tones and difference tones, or intermodulation products. The most commonly heard of these tones is that known as the primary or first-order difference tone. For two tones with frequencies f_1 and f_2, the frequency of the first-order difference tone is $(f_2 - f_1)$, where f_2 is the higher frequency. Thus, the frequency of the first-order difference tone is higher for wider intervals and lower for narrower intervals. For the first-order difference tone to be heard, the difference of the two parent tones must be greater than c. 25 Hz – 30 Hz. When the difference between the parent frequencies is less than an octave, the first-order difference tone is lower than either of the parent frequencies. When the parent frequencies are separated by more than an octave, the first-order difference tone appears between the two parent frequencies. In the latter case, the first-order difference tone is very difficult to detect.

In addition to the first-order difference tone, other, higher-order difference tones are sometimes detected. The most frequently heard of these have the frequencies

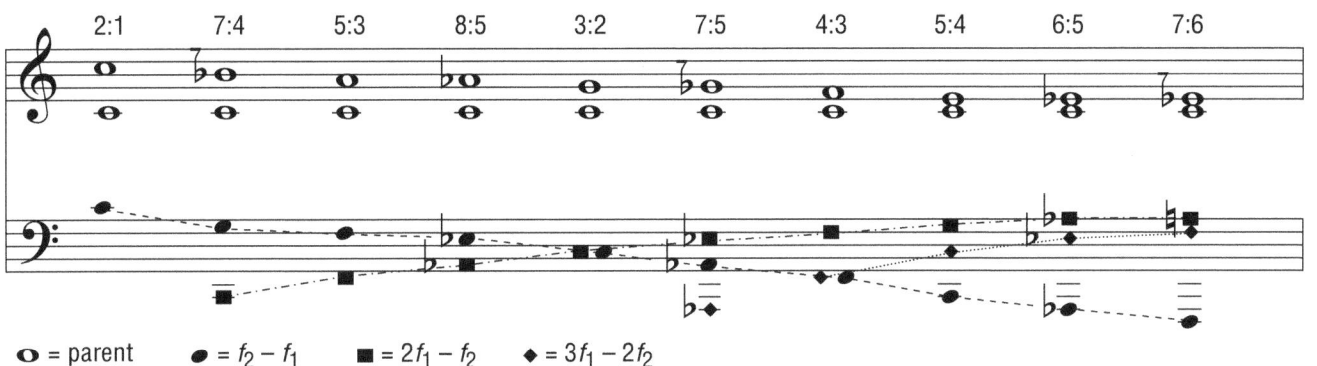

Figure 2.10: Difference tones of simple-ratio intervals

○ = parent ● = $f_2 - f_1$ ■ = $2f_1 - f_2$ ♦ = $3f_1 - 2f_2$

($2f_1 - f_2$) and ($3f_1 - 2f_2$). Unlike the first-order difference tone, these two tones are higher for narrower intervals and lower for wider intervals. Observe that both of these frequencies correspond to the differences between integer multiples of the parent frequencies. There is yet another class of combinational tones which have been the subject of considerable debate. These are the so-called summation tones. For parent tones with the frequencies f_1 and f_2, the first-order summation tone has the frequency ($f_2 + f_1$). Whereas difference tones, at least those of the first order, can be readily heard under normal listening conditions, summation tones are rarely detected by the listener, despite the fact that their components can be detected in the ear.

What is the musical significance of combination tones? Consider the intervals shown in Figure 2.10. Each of these intervals corresponds to a simple whole number ratio, and represents one of the basic consonances as defined in Just Intonation. In each case, the three most prominent combinational tones, *where present*, also form consonant intervals with both parent tones and with each other. Further, the combinational tones combine with the parent tones to form a portion of a harmonic series. In all but one case (8:5), one or more of the combinational tones corresponds to the fundamental of a harmonic series implied by the parent tones.

In contrast, intervals that are not simple integer ratios produce difference tones that are not harmonically related to the parent tones. For example, the frequency of the tempered middle C (assuming A = 440) is 261.62 Hz and the frequency of the E a tempered major third higher is 329.62 Hz. The difference between these two frequencies is 68 Hz. The frequency of the C two octaves below middle C is 65.41 Hz. The difference between these two frequencies is approximately two thirds of a semitone (near the point of maximum disturbance for interference beats). Hence, the first-order difference tone of the tempered major third conflicts with the lower tone of the interval, muddying the harmonic identity of the interval.

Periodicity Pitch

When two or more pure tones separated by intervals greater than the critical band are sounded simultaneously, the auditory mechanism is sensitive to the period or frequency of the resulting composite waveform. This gives rise to a phenomenon variously known as the periodicity pitch, virtual pitch, subjective pitch, residue tone, or the missing fundamental. We will use the term periodicity pitch, as this term most accurately identifies the source of the phenomenon. Musical consonance is associated with high periodicity pitch, which, as will be demonstrated below, is a property of intervals that can be represented by simple integer ratios.

For two pure tones with the frequencies f_1 and f_2, where $f_2 = m/n \times f_1$ and m and n are integers, the result is a relatively simple wave pattern with a period, τ_0, that is equal to $\tau_1 \times n$, where τ_1 is the period of the lower tone; and a frequency, f_0, that is equal to f_1/n. *The smaller the value of n, the shorter the period and the higher the frequency of the resulting pattern.* Figure 2.11 illustrates the composite wave patterns for a perfect fifth and perfect fourth. In the case of the perfect fifth, where $f_2 = 3/2 \times f_1$, the period of the composite waveform, τ_0, is twice the period of the lower tone, τ_1, and hence the frequency of this composite pattern is $1/2 f_1$, that is, an octave below the lower tone. In the case of the perfect fourth, where $f_2 = 4/3 \times f_1$, the composite period is three times the period of the lower tone and therefore, for a constant f_1, the periodicity pitch is lower, being in this case $1/3 f_1$ or a perfect twelfth below the lower tone. Figure 2.12 shows the periodicity pitches

Figure 2.11: Compound periods of a perfect fifth and a perfect fourth

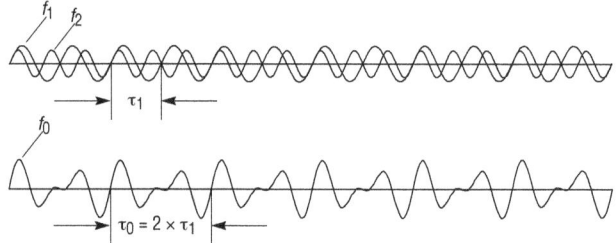

Perfect Fifth (3:2)

Perfect Fourth (4:3)

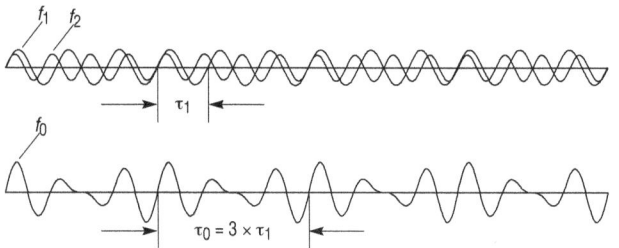

for a number of simple integer-ratio intervals, ranked in order of descending periodicity pitch. What is most significant about these periodicity pitches is that for any simple integer-ratio interval, the periodicity pitch corresponds to the fundamental of a harmonic series in which the generating tones correspond to the degrees designated by the numbers of the ratio. This accounts for the fact that only two or three low-numbered degrees of a harmonic series are required to give an impression of the fundamental. Although *any* pair of tones having a frequency ratio corresponding to consecutive degrees of a harmonic series has a repetition rate corresponding to the fundamental of that harmonic series, not all such pairs produce an unambiguous *sensation* of periodicity pitch corresponding to that repetition rate. It is gener-

ally held that unambiguous periodicity pitch is limited to ratios of integers no larger than 8 or 9. Pairs of tones corresponding to higher integer ratios generally have ambiguous periodicity pitches. The periodicity pitch of such an interval is generally an approximation of that of the nearest simple interval.

Observe that, for many simple-ratio intervals, the periodicity pitch is equivalent to the first-order difference tone. However, whereas difference tones are the products of nonlinearity of the inner and middle ear, periodicity pitch appears to be the result of higher-order neural processing. Evidence for this view includes the fact that frequencies corresponding to the difference tones can be measured in the cochlear fluid, whereas periodicity pitch cannot. Also, periodicity pitch can be heard even when the ear is saturated with a noise signal that masks the frequency range in which the tone occurs. Difference tones cannot be heard under these circumstances. Most conclusively, periodicity pitch is present even when the two components are presented dichotically to the two ears by means of headphones.

The question of how periodicity pitch is perceived has not as yet been conclusively answered. Periodicity pitch theories generally fall into two categories, which are described as "place" theories and "timing" theories. Place theories assume that the brain responds to the pattern of resonance regions on the basilar membrane produced by a group of pure tones that correspond to low-numbered degrees of a harmonic series. Timing theories assume that the brain detects the periodicity of nerve impulses produced by groups of pure tones with high periodicity pitches. Regardless of their time or place orientation, most recent theories of periodicity pitch hold that the pattern of the first seven or eight harmonic partials and their association with the pitch of the fundamental is either built into the human brain

Figure 2.12: Periodicity pitches of just intervals

o = parent tones   • = periodicity pitch

by evolution or learned early in life in the process of learning to recognize and decode human speech. This pattern serves as a sort of template to which sounds are compared. Any sound stimulus that provides a good match for two or more of the harmonics is assumed to produce the sensation of the fundamental.

COMPLEX TONES WITH HARMONIC PARTIALS

The complex tones that carry pitch information in most music consist of some number of harmonic or nearly harmonic partials. Instruments that produce sounds that can be indefinitely sustained, such as the human voice, the various wind instruments, and the bowed strings, generally produce partials that are strictly harmonic, whereas plucked or struck strings produce partials that are nearly harmonic, but include some measurable inharmonicity. (The amount of inharmonicity in a plucked or struck string is a product of its stiffness—the longer, thinner, and/or tauter a string is, the more nearly its partials will approximate a perfect harmonic series.) With a few exceptions, drums and those percussion instruments based on rods, bars, or plates (which musicologists categorize as idiophones) produce partials that are extremely inharmonic, bearing no recognizable relation to the harmonic series. The discussion that follows does not apply to instruments of these latter types.

Whereas the harmonic series, like the series of integers, is theoretically infinite, the series of partials making up any complex musical tone is finite. The number of partials present in a given tone, their relative intensities, and the way their intensities vary over time are the primary determinants of the musical property known as timbre or tone color. The relative intensities of the different partials making up a given complex tone are referred to as the *harmonic spectrum* of that tone. As will be explained below, harmonic partials have a significant effect on the consonance of musical intervals, so the presence or absence of a particular partial in the spectrum of a given instrument will have an effect on the quality of certain intervals played on that instrument.

The harmonic spectra of the various woodwind and brass instruments are quite complex and varied, and a detailed discussion of these phenomena is outside the scope of this publication. However, we can make a few useful generalizations. The conical-bored instruments (all of the brasses and all reeds except the clarinet) have harmonic spectra that are complete (that is, all of the integer multiples of the fundamental are present) up to a certain characteristic *cutoff frequency*, which varies from instrument to instrument. Typically, partials at least as high as the sixteenth make significant contributions to the timbres of these instruments. The relative intensities of the partials vary not just from instrument to instrument, but from register to register in a given instrument. The reed instruments in particular, have harmonic spectra that are quite "lumpy"; characteristic resonances known as *formants* reinforce partials in particular frequency ranges, regardless of the fundamental frequency of the tone being sounded. The clarinet is unique in having a spectrum, at least in the lower register, in which only the odd members of the harmonic series have a significant role. The tone of flutes is characterized by only the lowest few harmonics. In all of the wind instruments, an increase in overall intensity can be expected to result in an increase in the relative intensity of the higher partials. Particularly in the case of the reed instruments, the ability of the player to vary the relative intensity of the higher partials independently of the overall intensity is an important aspect of expressive playing.

In the plucked or struck strings, the relative intensities of the partials decrease in a predictable manner as the partial number increases. In the case of a plucked string, the relative intensities are inversely proportional to the square of the partial number; that is, the second partial is one-fourth as strong as the fundamental, the third is one-ninth as strong as the fundamental, the fourth is one-sixteenth as strong as the fundamental, and so on. In the case of a struck string, the relative intensities of the higher partials are greater, being inversely proportional to the partial number rather than its square. In this case the second partial is one-half the intensity of the fundamental, the third partial is one-third the intensity of the fundamental, and so on. In the case of either plucked or struck strings, the higher partials typically die away ("decay") more rapidly than the lower partials.

When two or more complex tones with harmonic partials are sounded simultaneously, we have the equivalent of many simultaneous simple tones. All of the phenomena described previously that result from the interaction of two pure tones can also result from the various pairs of components that exist when two complex tones are heard together, and can therefore be assumed to play some role in shaping the perception of these phenomena. Difference tones are most likely to be heard between the fundamentals of complex tones because the funda-

Table 2.2: Beats of a mistuned unison

Harmonic	Tone 1 (Hz)	Tone 2 (Hz)	f_B (Hz)
1	500	501	1
2	1000	1002	2
3	1500	1503	3
4	2000	2004	4
5	2500	2505	5
6	3000	3006	6
7	3500	3507	7
8	4000	4008	8

mentals usually have the greatest intensity. Difference tones between some of the stronger harmonics can also sometimes be detected, although difference tones produced by higher harmonics are likely to be masked by lower harmonics. Recent research on periodicity pitch indicates that complex tones as well as simple tones are capable of manifesting this phenomenon.

COINCIDENT OR BEATING HARMONICS

The aspect of relationships between simultaneously sounded complex tones with harmonic partials that has attracted the most attention among theorists is the coincidence of certain harmonics when pairs of complex tones are tuned in simple-ratio intervals, or conversely, the presence of beats resulting from the noncoincidence of these same partials when pairs of complex tones deviate from these simple intervals.

We have already examined the effect of beats between simple tones. To summarize, beats take place between two simple tones whose frequencies are near unison.

Table 2.3: Alignment of the harmonics in a properly tuned octave

Tone 1		Tone 2	
Harmonic	Frequency (Hz)	Harmonic	Frequency (Hz)
1	500	—	—
2	1000	1	1000
3	1500	—	—
4	2000	2	2000
5	2500	—	—
6	3000	3	3000
7	3500	—	—
8	4000	4	4000

These beats occur at a rate that is the difference in Hz between the two generating frequencies. Beats can be perceived clearly when the difference is less than 20 Hz–25 Hz, but as the difference increases beyond this point the beats blend together, giving rise to a general sensation of roughness. This roughness gradually decreases as the difference increases, persisting until the difference exceeds the critical band, which, for most of the audio range falls between a whole tone and a minor third.

These same principles apply to beats arising from partials (harmonic or otherwise) of complex tones. To take the simplest case, consider a unison between two tones having a complete set of harmonic partials. For the present discussion, let us give both of these tones a frequency of 500 Hz. When the two tones are tuned in exact unison, every harmonic of the first tone corresponds to the equivalent harmonic of the second. The resulting blend is absolutely smooth and free from any disturbance. Now let us detune one of the tones by 1 Hz. What is the result? The two fundamentals will now beat at a frequency of 501 − 500 = 1 Hz. That is not all, however. When the fundamentals are mistuned, each and every pair of harmonics is also mistuned, as can be seen in Table 2.2. Since the frequencies of the two second harmonics are 1000 Hz and 1002 Hz, they will beat at a frequency of 2 Hz, the two third harmonics, having frequencies of 1500 Hz and 1503 Hz, will beat at 3 Hz. Each successive pair of harmonics will beat at a rate that is an integer multiple of the beat frequency of the fundamentals.

Consider now the case of the octave (ratio 2:1). When two complex tones with harmonic partials are tuned in a perfect 2:1 ratio, every second harmonic of the lower tone matches a harmonic of the higher tone,

Table 2.4: Beats of a mistuned octave

Tone 1		Tone 2		
Harmonic	Frequency (Hz)	Harmonic	Frequency (Hz)	f_B
1	500	—	—	—
2	1000	1	1002	2
3	1500	—	—	—
4	2000	2	2004	4
5	2500	—	—	—
6	3000	3	3006	6
7	3500	—	—	—
8	4000	4	4008	8

Figure 2.13: Matching harmonics of just consonances

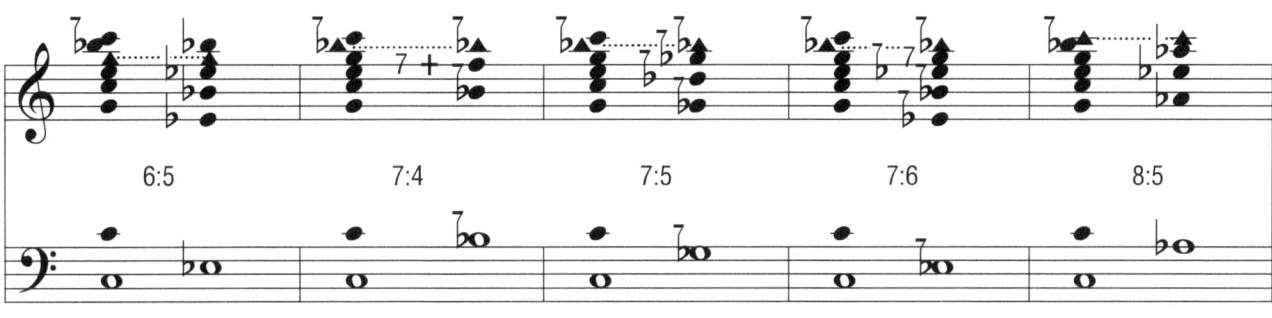

O = fundamenal ● = harmonic ▲ = matched harmonic

as in Table 2.3. If one of the tones is detuned slightly, beating again results. In this case (Table 2.4) the beats occur between the second harmonic of the lower tone and the fundamental of the higher, the fourth harmonic of the lower tone and the second of the higher, and so on. Hence, there are only half the number of beating pairs as are produced by a mistuned unison. Again, the beat frequencies are integer multiples of the difference between the second harmonic of the lower tone and the fundamental of the higher.

For any interval of the form $n:1$, where n is an integer, every harmonic of the higher tone will be matched by the harmonic of the lower tone which has its number multiplied by n. Any difference tones present will also correspond to harmonics of the lower tone. The periodicity pitch also corresponds to the pitch of the lower tone. In these cases, the higher tone, if accurately tuned, contributes no new information, but merely reinforces selected harmonics of the lower.[7] Provided that the lower tone is not so low in frequency that its harmonics beat with one another, the harmonics of the higher tone cannot beat with those of the lower.[8] If such an interval is detuned from its simple-ratio ideal, beats will occur between the detuned pairs of partials, and potentially between various pairs of difference tones.

When two tones are in a whole-number ratio interval that is not of the type described above, the numbers of the ratio indicate the lowest pair of harmonics that will match between the two tones. For any integer ratio of the form m:n, where m represents the higher tone, the mth harmonic of the lower tone and the nth harmonic of the higher tone will coincide. For example, in the case of the perfect fifth (ratio 3:2), the third harmonic of the lower tone matches the second harmonic of the higher tone. In the case of the perfect fourth, (ratio 4:3) the fourth harmonic of the lower tone matches the third harmonic of the higher tone. Higher harmonics that are integer multiples of the lowest matching pair will, of course, also match, for example, in the case of the perfect fifth, 6:4, 9:6, 12:8, and so on. Several of the principal consonances with their matching harmonics are illustrated in Figure 2.13. (The matching harmonics are represented by triangular noteheads joined by dotted horizontal lines.) When any of these simple consonances is mistuned, the matched harmonics form mistuned unisons and beats are generated at a frequency correspond-

Table 2.5: Alignment of the harmonics of a just perfect fifth

Tone 1		Tone 2	
Harmonic	Frequency (Hz)	Harmonic	Frequency (Hz)
1	500	—	—
—	—	1	750
2	1000	—	—
3	**1500**	**2**	**1500**
4	2000	—	—
—	—	3	2250
5	2500	—	—
6	**3000**	**4**	**3000**
7	3500	—	—
—	—	5	3750
8	4000	—	—

Table 2.6: Beats of a mistuned perfect fifth

Tone 1		Tone 2		
Harmonic	Frequency (Hz)	Harmonic	Frequency (Hz)	f_B
1	500	—	—	—
—	—	1	752	—
2	1000	—	—	—
3	**1500**	**2**	**1504**	**4**
4	2000	—	—	—
—	—	3	2256	—
5	2500	—	—	—
6	**3000**	**4**	**3008**	**8**
7	3500	—	—	—
—	—	5	3760	—
8	4000	—	—	—

ing to the difference between the frequencies of the harmonics in question. This fact provides an essential cue for tuning any of these simple consonances by ear on instruments producing harmonic or nearly harmonic partials. One simply listens for and eliminates the beats between the defining pair of harmonics.

Table 2.5 shows the frequencies of the first eight harmonics of the lower tone and the first five harmonics of the higher tone for two tones forming a perfect fifth. When the two tones form a perfect 3:2, the third harmonic of the lower tone and the second harmonic of the higher tone correspond exactly, as do the sixth harmonic of the lower tone and the fourth of the higher. When the fundamental of the higher tone is raised by 2 Hz, as in Table 2.6, the harmonics of the higher tone are mistuned proportionally and beats occur between the third harmonic of the lower tone and the second harmonic of the higher tone at 4 Hz, and between the sixth harmonic of the lower tone and the fourth harmonic of the higher tone at 8 Hz.

The set of intervals that can be tuned by eliminating beats from one or more pairs of harmonic partials extends beyond the perfect fifth to embrace all of the intervals conventionally recognized as consonances in common-practice theory, as well as some additional intervals not so recognized. As the ordinal numbers of the lowest defining pair of partials increase, the number of matching pairs and their relative intensities decrease, while the likelihood of interference from other, nonmatching pairs of harmonics increases. Eventually, the strength of the matching partials decreases and the roughness from other sources increases until, somewhere in the vicinity of the eighth or ninth harmonic, it is no longer possible to distinguish when the defining partials have reached a perfect unison, and hence, the interval cannot be confidently tuned by "zero beating" the defining harmonics.

ARTHUR H. BENADE'S "SPECIAL RELATIONSHIPS"

In his excellent book, *The Fundamentals of Musical Acoustics*, Physicist and flutist Arthur H. Benade describes an experiment that he frequently performed with his students that gives an accurate picture of the role played by beats as cues for tuning simple-ratio intervals between sustained tones with harmonic partials.[9] Benade used two audio oscillators that were constructed so as to produce tones with three or four exactly harmonic partials of appreciable strength. One oscillator is tuned to a fixed frequency somewhere in the range of 250 Hz – 1,000 Hz (C_4–C_6). A volunteer is then invited to tune the second oscillator up or down until he or she finds a setting which produces a "special relationship," which Benade describes as "a beat-free setting, narrowly confined between two restricted regions in which a wide variety of beats take place." According to Benade, experiments of this type consistently identified as special relationships those intervals listed in Table 2.7. As those who are familiar with theories of Just Intonation will immediately recognize, and those who are not will discover in the course of subsequent chapters, the intervals in the table are precisely those that are almost universally regarded as consonances by advocates of

Just Intonation. It is particularly notable that, in addition to intervals commonly regarded as consonances (albeit in their tempered versions) by conventional music theory, the table includes three ratios involving seven (7:4, 7:5, and 7:6) that are not recognized in conventional music theory. Indeed, 7:4 is in the vicinity of the tempered minor seventh (1000 cents) and 7:5 is even closer to the tempered tritone (600 cents), both intervals that conventional theory identifies as dissonances. It is apparent, therefore, that the experimenters are not simply picking out intervals that are familiar as consonances from their musical training but are really responding to the special physical properties of these particular whole-number ratio intervals.

Equally revealing is the reaction Benade got from his students when he retuned the variable oscillator from one of the special integer relationships to a nearby tempered interval normally accepted as a consonance. When, for example, he substituted the tempered major third (400 cents, approximately 1.25992:1) for the just 5:4, all of the musicians in the room agreed that the interval was "an out of tune (sharp) major third." His listeners "typically react with skepticism or dismay" when they are told that the out-of-tune interval they are hearing is a correctly tuned major third from the perspective of the culturally dominant system. "What," they ask, "makes anyone think that those are acceptable tunings?" Benade goes on to explain that laboratory oscillators are unlike musical instruments, and that real instruments meet with varying degrees of success in trying to replicate the intervals discovered in the experiment. He suggests that there are a variety of reasons that musicians might choose to deviate from these whole-number "special relationships." Nevertheless, his experiment clearly illustrates that the intervals of Just Intonation have distinct perceptual qualities that can be recognized by listeners without special training (or even, in the case of trained musicians, despite special training).

It is worth noting that Benade's experiments were conducted with frequencies located in the two octaves above middle C, and that his special relationships are not necessarily "beat free" when played in lower registers. If the defining pair of harmonics is tuned in perfect unison, they will, of course, not generate beats, regardless of the register. However, other nonmatching pairs of harmonics may form narrow enough intervals to set up beats. In the perfect fourth, for example, the third harmonic of the lower tone and the second of the higher form a major second. In the major third, the fourth harmonic of the lower tone and the third harmonic of the higher tone form a minor second. In the minor third, the fifth harmonic of the lower tone and the fourth of the higher form the same interval. Other narrow intervals can be found between one or more pairs of noncoincident harmonics in the remaining intervals in Figure 2.13. Whether these close intervals introduce beats or roughness in these otherwise consonant intervals depends on the absolute frequencies of the tones concerned. In any case, their presence does not prevent these intervals from being accurately tuned by the elimination of beats from the identifying harmonics. Neither do they appear to seriously mar the perceived consonance of the intervals, except, perhaps, in relatively low registers.

It is my experience from experiments with tones such as those used by Benade that his list of special relationships is more or less complete as far as intervals smaller than an octave are concerned. The only other interval that might be included in the set is 8:7 (231.2 cents), a wide major second known in Just Intonation parlance as the supermajor second or septimal major second. However, this interval is narrow enough that the fundamentals beat in the lower and middle registers. The resulting roughness makes it extremely difficult to match the usually much weaker seventh and eighth harmonics by eliminating beats. Hence, 8:7 stands on the border between consonance and dissonance.

Special Relationships Beyond the Octave

If we repeat Benade's experiment, allowing the variable tone to move over a more extended range, we can expand the list of special relationships to include a number of intervals wider than the octave. These include, in order

Table 2.7: Arthur Benade's "special relationships"

Rank	Ratio	Name
1	2:1	Octave
2	3:2	Perfect Fifth
3	4:3	Perfect Fourth
4	5:3	Major Sixth
5	5:4	Major Third
6	6:5	Minor Third
7	7:4	Harmonic or Septimal Minor Seventh
8	7:5	Septimal Tritone
9	8:5	Minor Sixth
10	7:6	Subminor or Septimal Minor Third

of increasing size, the following octave extensions of the previously encountered special relationships: 7:3 (the septimal or subminor tenth), 5:2 (the major tenth), 8:3 (the octave extension of the perfect fourth), 3:1 (the perfect twelfth), 7:2 (the octave extension of the harmonic seventh), 4:1 (the double octave), 5:1 (two octaves plus a major third), 6:1 (two octaves plus a perfect fifth), 7:1 (two octaves plus a harmonic seventh), and, marginally, 8:1 (the triple octave). Special relationships among tones separated by intervals greater than three octaves can only be detected if the lower tone has a great many strong upper harmonics. Such a timbre would be characterized as "reedy" or "nasal," and would have limited musical applications. The list of special relationships wider than the octave, like the list compiled by Benade, does not include any ratios with numerators larger than eight. This excludes the octave extensions of several intervals that are normally regarded as consonant, such as the minor third (6:5, octave extension 12:5), the minor sixth (8:5, octave extension 16:5), and the major sixth (5:3, octave extension 10:3). Hence, it cannot be assumed that because an interval in close form is consonant, all of its octave extensions are also necessarily consonant. An additional interval that is not an octave extension of one of the previously defined special relationships, but which is marginally consonant, is 9:4, the major ninth.

On the Consonance of Relationships Involving Higher Harmonics

All of the special relationships discovered by Benade, as well as the wider intervals enumerated above, are defined by pairs of partials that fall in the first three octaves of the harmonic series (harmonic numbers 1–8). Further, every interval smaller than an octave that is defined by a pair of harmonics within the first three octaves of the series, with the possible exception of 8:7, qualifies as a special relationship.

If we examine the fourth octave of the series (harmonics 8–16), we find a great many more integer ratios which one might expect to qualify as special relationships if the experiment was conducted using a timbre with more high harmonics than that used by Benade. However, this generally proves not to be the case. Using a timbre with sixteen or more harmonics, with the relative intensities of the harmonics decreasing as their ordinal numbers increase (a timbre that would be described as "reedy" or "nasal") I can detect no "still points" that mark the exact tuning of any of these intervals, such as are easily detected for all of Benade's special relationships. The absence of such still points is explained by the fact that every interval that depends for its definition on a pair of harmonics in the range 8–16 also includes one or more lower (and hence more prominent) pairs of harmonics which will form an interval smaller than a semitone (in the region that produces the maximum roughness) when the defining pair is tuned in a perfect unison. Any increased smoothness contributed to one of these intervals by bringing the defining pair of harmonics into unison is offset, and probably masked, by the increased roughness contributed by the mistuning of the lower pair(s). Widening or narrowing these intervals slightly may result in an increase in roughness from some sources and a decrease from others, but an unmistakable cessation of roughness is achieved only by moving away from one of these intervals and approaching one of the simpler intervals defined by lower harmonics. What was said above about intervals based on the harmonics 8–16 is even more applicable to intervals defined by harmonics above 16. The higher you go up the harmonic series, the closer together the harmonics become. The number of potential interfering harmonics in any region increases accordingly, whereas the relative intensities of the defining harmonics typically decrease as their ordinal numbers increase.

Although I have found no special relationships smaller than the octave based on the harmonics 8–16, I have found a significant number of such intervals wider than the octave. Using a fixed, lower tone with a timbre that has strong harmonics as high as 16, and a timbre with fewer high harmonics for the higher movable tone, octave extensions of several of the intervals involving the fourth octave of the harmonic series can be identified as special relationships. These include 11:5, 11:4, 11:3, 11:2, 11:1, 13:6, 13:5, 13:4, 13:3, 13:2, and 13:1. The reason these intervals are identifiable as special relationships, whereas the more compact forms are not, is that in all of these cases, the defining harmonic supplied by the higher tone falls in the first three octaves of the harmonic series, and hence the conflicting harmonics of the lower tone are displaced into the octaves *above* the defining pair of harmonics for the interval. It should be noted, however, that the timbre required to identify these ratios of eleven and thirteen as special relationships is quite strident and very fatiguing to listen to for extended periods. It is doubtful that anyone would want to create an entire composition using such a timbre.

BASIC DEFINITIONS, CONVENTIONS, AND PROCEDURES

INTRODUCTION

In Just Intonation, musical intervals are expressed as ratios of whole numbers. In order to acquire a clear understanding of Just Intonation, one must learn to manipulate such ratios. This point cannot be overemphasized. The ability to perform calculations on ratios and understand the musical implications of the results is as important as the ability to hear and recognize the intervals that the ratios represent. In order to obtain the maximum benefit from this primer, you cannot simply accept "on faith" the mathematical relations among pitches, intervals, scales, and chords that are described herein. You must perform the necessary calculations yourself in order to understand how the results were obtained. Fortunately, the level of mathematics required to understand Just Intonation is elementary. All that is required is simple arithmetic, the mastery of a few simple rules, and occasional recourse to an inexpensive scientific calculator.

RULES AND CONVENTIONS

Certain conventions should be observed in handling musical ratios. While some of these conventions are essentially arbitrary, they are useful in avoiding confusion.[1]

1. Unless stated otherwise, ratios are always expressed in least terms. That is, any common factors in the denominator and the numerator are canceled.

2. The numerator (over number) of a ratio always represents the higher of the two tones delineating an interval. In other words, the numerator of a just ratio will always be greater than the denominator. For example, a perfect fifth will always be expressed as 3:2, never as 2:3. (One exception to this rule will be found when scales are presented in staff notation. When a ratio representing the interval between two successive scale tones is placed between those two tones on the staff, the higher number will be placed closest to the higher pitch.)

3. Ratios are used for two different purposes in Just Intonation: to represent intervals, and to represent specific pitches. In this book, we will differentiate these two functions by using the colon to denote intervals and the slash to denote pitches. For example, the ratio 3:2 represents a just perfect fifth — any just perfect fifth whatever, regardless of which two tones it occurs between. On the other hand, $3/2$ represents a specific pitch, that which is a perfect fifth (3:2) above $1/1$. Thus, if $1/1$ represents C, then $3/2$ represents the G a perfect fifth above C.[2] Note that this convention is not followed by Partch or by other any other writers on Just Intonation that I am aware of. However, it is usually easy enough to distinguish from context whether ratios represent pitches or intervals.

4. When a ratio is used to represent a tone rather than an interval, it is always "octaved." That is, the ratio is always expressed in the form it has in the octave between $1/1$ and $2/1$, regardless of what register it actually falls in. For example, if C is $1/1$, then the G a perfect fifth higher will always be represented as $3/2$, regardless of what register the G falls in. When speaking of intervals, it is of course both necessary and appropriate to use ratios representing intervals greater than 2:1. For example, 3:2 represents a perfect fifth, whereas 3:1 represents a perfect twelfth; 9:8 represents a major second, whereas 9:4 represents a major ninth.

CALCULATIONS WITH RATIOS

ADDITION

As stated above, calculations involving just intervals are simple. To add two intervals, multiply their ratios. For example, 3:2 + 9:8 = (3 × 9):(2 × 8) = 27:16; 3:2 + 4:3 = (3 × 4):(2 × 3) = 12:6 = 2:1. Note that in the second example, an additional step was required to reduce the ratio to its least terms.

SUBTRACTION

To subtract one interval from another, invert the ratio representing the interval to be subtracted, then multiply.

For example, $3:2 - 9:8 = (3 \times 8):(2 \times 9) = 24:18 = 4:3$; $3:2 - 4:3 = (3 \times 3):(2 \times 4) = 9:8$.

If we are dealing with tones and addition results in a ratio greater than $2/1$ (that is, a ratio in which the numerator is greater than twice the denominator) simply subtract one or more 2:1s as necessary to obtain the proper result: $3/2 + 7:4 = (7 \times 3)/(2 \times 4) = 21/8$; $21/8 - 2:1 = 21/(2 \times 8) = 21/16$. Similarly, if subtraction results in a ratio less than $1/1$ (that is, a ratio with a denominator greater than its numerator), add the appropriate number of 2:1s: $9/8 - 27:16 = (9 \times 16)/(27 \times 8) = 144/216 = 2/3$; $2/3 + 2:1 = (2 \times 2)/3 = 4/3$.

Complementation

An interval's *complement* is that interval which, when added to said interval, yields an octave (2:1). Every just interval less than an octave has a complement. For example, the complement of 3:2 is 4:3, since $3:2 + 4:3 = 12:6 = 2:1$. To find the complement of any interval smaller than an octave, subtract that interval from 2:1. Expressing the same idea in a slightly different way, tuning a particular interval, which we will call *x:y*, *upward* from $1/1$ will generate the same tone (assuming octave equivalency) as tuning its complement, *2y:x*, *downward* from $2/1$. Thus, tuning a 3:2 above C and tuning a 4:3 below C both yield the same tone, G $3/2$ (albeit in different octaves). Several pairs of complementary intervals are shown in Figure 3.1.

It is also possible (and sometimes useful) to complement a chord or a scale. This is done by replacing each tone of the chord or scale with its complement (that is, the tone related to $1/1$ by the complementary interval). For example, consider the just C major scale illustrated in Figure 3.2. To complement the scale, complement each of the ratios ($1/1$ and $2/1$ are considered each other's complements). The result is the descending C Phrygian/F minor scale: $2/1$, $16/9$, $8/5$, $3/2$, $4/3$, $6/5$, $16/15$, $1/1$. Don't worry at this point about the particular ratios that compose these two scales. The important concept to grasp here is that complementing a scale gives a scale with the same pattern of intervals occurring in reverse order.

Converting Ratios to Cents

To compare the magnitudes of just intervals, or to compare just intervals with those of equal temperament or other nonrational systems, it is necessary to convert just ratios to *cents*. (This is where the above-mentioned scientific calculator comes in handy.) The cent is a logarithmic unit of measure invented by the nineteenth century British physicist Alexander J. Ellis. One cent equals $1/100$ of an equally tempered semitone or $1/1200$ of an octave. To find the number of cents in an interval, convert the ratio to decimal form, then find its logarithm. (Either common or natural logarithms may be used. Here, we will use common (base 10) logs). Next, multiply the result by $1200/\log 2$. 3986.3 is a sufficiently accurate approximation of $1200/\log 2$ for most purposes. For example, $3:2 = 1.5$; $\log 1.5 = 0.1760913$; $\times 3986.3 = 701.95$ cents. The more accurate the approximations of the log of the ratio and $1200/\log 2$ are, the more accurate will be the result. Speaking practically, however, accuracy greater than ±0.01 cent is seldom required. Intervals expressed in cents are subject to all of the operations of ordinary arithmetic.

Dividing Just Intervals

Musicians trained in conventional theory are accustomed to being able to divide tempered intervals into some number of equal parts. For example, the octave can be divided equally into two tempered tritones (augmented fourths/diminished fifths) three tempered major thirds, four tempered minor thirds, and six tempered whole tones. And every tempered interval is evenly

Figure 3.1: Some pairs of complementary intervals

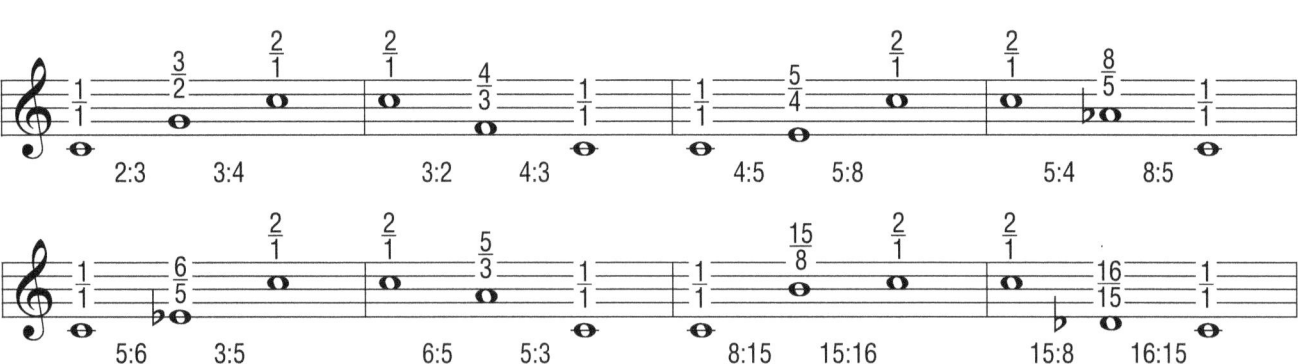

divisible into some number of tempered semitones. In Just Intonation, no *simple* interval is divisible into any number of *equal* parts. To be sure, all just intervals can be divided into any number of parts whatever, but except for certain rather complex intervals that will be described below, they can only be divided *un*equally.

The simplest possible divisions of any just interval are implicit in the ratio that represents said interval. Consider the octave, 2:1. To divide 2:1 into two parts, multiply both terms of the interval by 2 to obtain the equivalent ratio 4:2, then interpolate the missing integer in the series, 3, to obtain 4:3:2. This indicates that the simplest division of 2:1 yields the perfect fourth (4:3) and the perfect fifth (3:2). To divide 2:1 into three parts, multiply both terms by 3 to obtain 6:3, then interpolate the two missing integers (5 and 4) to obtain the series 6:5:4:3. This indicates that the simplest division of the octave into three parts yields a minor third (6:5), a major third (5:4) and a perfect fourth (4:3). To divide the octave into four parts, multiply the terms by 4 and interpolate the three missing integers to obtain the series 8:7:6:5:4. The simplest division of the octave into four parts yields the major third and minor third again, plus two unfamiliar intervals, the septimal or supermajor second (8:7) and the septimal minor or subminor third (7:6). These latter two intervals constitute the simplest possible division for the perfect fourth into two parts (4:3 = 8:6), whereas the former two constitute the simplest possible division of the perfect fifth (3:2 = 6:4). One can continue this process indefinitely, dividing the octave into any number of unequal parts using ratios of increasing complexity. The resulting intervals can have their positions shuffled within the octave, and the smaller intervals can be recombined in various ways to create yet other divisions of the octave. The procedure described above can be applied to all ratios of the form x+1:x, which are known as *superparticular* ratios. This category includes the majority of the most significant just intervals.

Ratios that are not superparticular can be readily divided simply by interpolating the missing integers between the two terms. For example, the major sixth, 5:3, is divisible into 5:4 and 4:3. The minor sixth, 8:5, is divisible into 8:7, 7:6, and 6:5. The harmonic seventh, 7:4, is divisible into 7:6, 6:5, and 5:4. It is, of course, possible to divide such nonsuperparticular ratios into a greater number of parts by multiplying the terms of the ratio by any integer then interpolating the missing integers in the series as was done above with the superparticular intervals. For example, 5:3 multiplied by 2 becomes 10:6, and is then divisible into 10:9, 9:8, 8:7, and 7:6.

The process of division described above inevitably results in the inclusion of higher prime factors as an interval is divided into a greater number of parts. As will become clear in later chapters, it is often desirable to obtain the simplest division of an interval into a given number of parts within a given *prime limit*. Consider, for example, the division of the octave into four parts described above, which yielded the intervals 8:7, 7:6, 6:5, and 5:4. This division involves the prime factors 2, 3, 5, and 7. Suppose, however, one wished to divide the octave into four parts without involving the prime number 7. In this case, it is necessary to multiply the terms of the ratio by larger integers and discard the terms that are above the desired prime limit. To divide the octave into four parts while remaining within the five limit, multiplying by either five or six will produce the same results. Multiplying by five yields the series 10:9:8:7:6:5. Deleting the seven yields the intervals 10:9, 9:8, 4:3 (8:6), 6:5. Multiplying by six yields the series 12:11:10:9:8:7:6. Deleting eleven and seven yields 6:5, 10:9, 9:8, 4:3 (8:6), which includes the same four intervals as the previous series, but in a different order.

Figure 3.2: Two complementary scales

The only whole-number ratio intervals that can be divided into two equal parts which are also whole-number ratio intervals are those in which both terms are perfect squares, such as 4:1 (2:1 + 2:1), 9:4 (3:2 + 3:2), 16:9 (4:3 + 4:3), 25:16 (5:4 + 5:4), 36:25 (6:5 + 6:5), and the like. Similarly, the only intervals that can be divided into three equal parts are those in which both terms are perfect cubes, such as 8:1, 27:8, 64:27, and the like. One can carry this process on indefinitely, dividing ratios composed of higher powers of integers into larger numbers of equal parts, but the intervals that result do not seem to have any particular musical significance. The simple intervals that are capable of only unequal division are much more important than those few which are capable of equal division.

Calculating Absolute Frequencies (Hz)

As stated previously, Just Intonation is concerned with precise relations between pitches rather than with absolute frequencies or pitches. As a result, you will find few representations of pitches expressed as frequencies in Hz (Hertz) in the remainder of this primer. However, if you require frequencies in Hz, in order, for example, to tune an instrument by means of a frequency counter, it is a simple matter to convert just tones designated by ratios to absolute frequencies in Hz once you have decided what absolute frequency to assign to $1/1$. In my own compositions, I normally designate $1/1$ as the pitch C, and assign middle C the frequency a 5:3 below A 440. Hence the frequency of middle C is $440 \times 3/5 = 264$ Hz. Given this standard, any other frequency related to $1/1$ by a ratio can be easily calculated by multiplication. For example, the frequency of the G a perfect fifth above middle C is $264 \times 3/2 = 396$ Hz. An E ($5/4$) a major tenth above middle C is $264 \times 5/2 = 660$ Hz. An F a perfect fifth *below* middle C is $264 \times 2/3 = 176$ Hz. In the last example, the frequency of middle C was multiplied by the inverse of the interval ($2/3$ rather than $3/2$) to find the frequency a 3:2 *below* $1/1$. The frequency of any tone whatever in any just system may be calculated with equal ease provided one has assigned some precise frequency to $1/1$.

The Harmonic Series and the Subharmonic Series

The harmonic series and the subharmonic series are two essential concepts for understanding Just Intonation. We have already encountered the harmonic series as the pattern of partials characterizing many musically useful timbres. However, the series can also be used to explain the relations between the pitches in a scale or chord. The harmonic series is the series of all of the integer multiples of some selected frequency f: (f, $2f$, $3f$, $4f$, $5f$...). The harmonic series is inherently an *ascending* series. The subharmonic series is the reciprocal or mirror image or complement of the harmonic series. It consists of all of the integer submultiples (divisions) of some selected frequency f: ($f/1$, $f/2$, $f/3$, $f/4$, $f/5$...). The subharmonic series is inherently a descending series. The first sixteen harmonics of C_2 and the first sixteen subharmonics of C_6 are illustrated in Figure 3.3.

Unlike the harmonic series, the subharmonic series is not represented in the partials of any known sounding bodies. Theorists in earlier centuries anxiously sought sounds in nature with subharmonic partials, but none were ever discovered.

Any interval in Just Intonation, taken in isolation, can be understood equally well as belonging to a harmonic series or a subharmonic series. For instance, the interval 3:2 can be understood either as part of a harmonic series beginning on an assumed fundamental an octave below the tone represented by 2, or it can be understood as $1/3:1/2$, part of a subharmonic series beginning on an assumed fundamental an octave above $1/2$. Just as an interval can be understood as belonging to either a harmonic or a subharmonic series, any chord, scale, or any concatenation of tones whatever in Just Intonation can be analyzed both as a segment of a harmonic series and as a segment of a subharmonic series, using the methods described below.

Converting Ratios to a Harmonic or Subharmonic Series Segment

To convert a series of tones represented by ratios to a series of integers representing degrees of a harmonic series, convert the ratios to their least common denominator, discard the denominators, and cancel any common factors shared by the numerators. First, prime factor the denominators. For example, in the case of the triad $16/15$, $4/3$, $8/5$, (D♭−, F, A♭) the denominators factor as 3×5, 3, and 5. Next, multiply together the highest powers of each of the primes found in the denominators to generate the common denominator: $3 \times 5 = 15$. Finally, multiply each of the numerators by the factors of the common denominator that are *not* factors of its original denominator: 16 (unchanged, because its original denominator is the same as the common denominator), $5 \times 4 = 20$, $3 \times 8 = 24$. Discarding the denominators, we

Figure 3.3: The first sixteen harmonics of C_2 and the first sixteen subharmonics of C_6

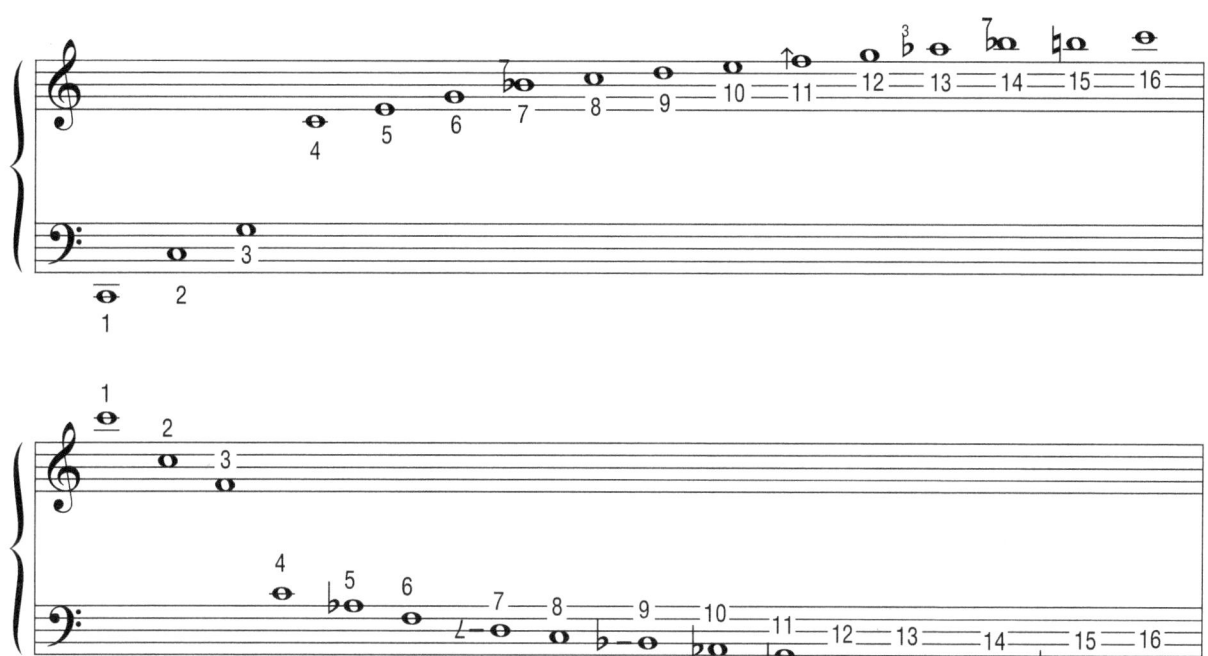

obtain the series 16:20:24. As a final step, we cancel any factors common to all of the numerators. In this case, we cancel the common factor 4, yielding the series 4:5:6 (a major triad in root position, as explained in the next chapter).

For a slightly more complex example, consider the series $9/5$, $9/8$, $27/20$, $63/40$ (B♭, D, F+, A♭+). As it happens, this series represents a dominant-seventh chord in root position. If we want to generate numbers that represent an ascending series, with $9/5$ (the root) at the bottom and $63/40$ (the seventh) at the top, we must make an exception to our usual practice of representing all just tones in the octave between C $1/1$ and C' $2/1$. As represented in the series above, $9/5$ is the highest of the four tones; to make it the lowest, we must either subtract $2/1$ from $9/5$ or add $2/1$ to the other three tones. Choosing the former option yields the series $9/10$, $9/8$, $27/20$, $63/40$. The denominators factor as (2×5), (2^3), $(2^2 \times 5)$, and $(2^3 \times 5)$, and the least common denominator is therefore $2^3 \times 5 = 40$. The resulting numerators are 36, 45, 54, and 63. When the common factor 9 is canceled from all of these numerators, the resulting series is 4:5:6:7, a just dominant-seventh chord.

To convert a series of tones represented by ratios to a series of integers corresponding to the degrees of a subharmonic series, convert the ratios to a least common numerator, discard the numerators, and cancel any common factors shared by the denominators. This procedure is analogous to that described above for converting a series of ratios to their least common denominator, except that the procedures applied to the denominators and numerators are exchanged. First, prime factor the numerators. For example, in the series $21/20$, $6/5$, $7/6$, the prime factors of the numerators are (3×7), (2×3), and 7, and the least common numerator is therefore 42 ($2 \times 3 \times 7$). Multiplying the denominators by the missing factors of their respective numerators yields the series 40:35:30. Eliminating the common factor 5 reduces the series to 8:7:6. Thus, the tones $21/20$, $6/5$, and $7/6$ correspond to degrees eight, seven, and six of a subharmonic series, of which $21/20$ is the fundamental (eight being an octave submultiple of the fundamental).

The relative significance of harmonic- and subharmonic-series concepts in generating and understanding just tuning systems is a matter of some controversy. Harry Partch, the best known Just Intonation theorist in the twentieth century, was a strong advocate for the equality of harmonic- and subharmonic-series based tonalities in Just Intonation, which he termed *otonalities* and *utonalities*, and a number of subsequent composers and theorists have subscribed to his view. It is my view that subharmonic tonalities must hold a secondary position, for reasons which I will explain in Chapter Four.

BASIC DEFINITIONS, CONVENTIONS, AND PROCEDURES

IDENTITIES

Ascending through a harmonic series (or descending through a subharmonic series), each new odd-numbered element we encounter represents a new tone that has not been heard previously, whereas each new even-numbered element represents an octave duplication of a previously heard pitch which was first encountered as an odd-numbered element. Consider the harmonic series segment illustrated in Figure 3.3. The first odd harmonic is C, the fundamental of the series. The second harmonic, which is, of course, even, is another C an octave above the fundamental. The third harmonic (odd) is a G a perfect twelfth (an octave plus a perfect fifth) above the fundamental. The fourth harmonic (even) is another C. The fifth harmonic (odd) is a new pitch, an E. The sixth harmonic (even) is an octave duplicate of 3, a G. The seventh harmonic (odd) is another new pitch, B♭ (a very flat B♭). The eighth harmonic (even) is yet another C. And so it goes: on, potentially, to infinity. Thus, in a harmonic series (or in a subharmonic series) it is only the odd numbered elements that represent unique pitches. When considered as components in a chord or tonality, the odd numbered degrees of a harmonic or subharmonic series are referred to as *identities*.

PRIME NUMBERS, PRIMARY INTERVALS, AND PRIME LIMITS

A prime number is an integer (positive whole number) that has as factors only itself and 1. All other integers can be expressed as unique products of primes, and so, therefore, can the integer ratios of Just Intonation. There is an infinite array of prime numbers, but only the first eight or so primes (2, 3, 5, 7, 11, 13, 17, 19) have *obvious* musical significance.[3] For each musically significant prime, there is a *primary interval* of the form $p:2^n$, where p is the prime and 2^n is the greatest power of 2 less than p. Thus, the primary intervals for the first eight primes are 2:1, 3:2, 5:4, 7:4, 11:8, 13:8, 17:16, and 19:16.[4] (These are *harmonic* primaries. From a subharmonic point of view, the primary interval would have the form $2^n:p$, with 2^n being the smallest power of 2 greater than p. In this case, the primary intervals for the first eight primes would be 2:1, 4:3, 8:5, 8:7, 16:11, 16:13, 32:17, and 32:19.)

It is customary to describe a given just scale or tuning system as belonging to a particular *prime limit*. If, for example, we say that a particular composition uses *five-limit* Just Intonation, we mean that only intervals based on the primes 2, 3, and 5 are involved. All of the possible intervals within a given prime limit can be explained as products of the primary intervals within that limit. Thus all of the possible intervals within the five limit can be explained as products of the primary intervals $2/1$, $3/2$, and $5/4$ (or of $2/1$, $4/3$, and $8/5$).

WHAT IS A CHORD?

In conventional music theory, a chord is defined as any group of three or more different pitches sounded simultaneously. A distinction is then made between consonant chords (the major and minor triads, with their various inversions) and dissonant chords (all other possible combinations). Chords are generally explained as being constructed by stacking thirds.

There is no universally recognized definition of a chord in Just Intonation, but a workable approximation might be something along the following lines: a group of three or more tones that correspond to relatively low-numbered identities of a harmonic (or subharmonic) series. This definition, like the definition of a consonance as an interval that can be represented by a relatively simple whole-number ratio, is imprecise, since it is not obvious where a line should be drawn either between simple and complex ratios, or between low and high-numbered identities. As stated previously, *any* possible concatenation of tones in a just tuning can be analyzed as a segment of either a harmonic or a subharmonic series. The essential characteristic of a just chord, as distinct from any other concatenation of tones which might arise in a just system, is that a chord is composed of a group of identities which are sufficiently low in the series and/or sufficiently numerous to allow the ear to deduce the fundamental of the series to which it belongs.[5] For example, a perfect fifth, consisting of the 1 and 3 identities of a tonality, is often sufficient to firmly establish that tonality, whereas a pair of higher identities, such as 5 and 7, would not establish the tonality nearly as firmly without the addition of further identities.

Table 3.1: Some voicings of a just C-major triad

Tones	Relative Frequencies	Identities
C, E, G	4:5:6	1–5–3
E, G, C'	5:6:8	5–3–1
G, C', E'	3:4:5	3–1–5
E, C', G'	5:8:12	5–1–3
G, E', C"	3:5:8	3–5–1
C, G, E'	2:3:5	1–3–5

In order to further distinguish true chords from all other concatenations of tones, I will propose two additional, interrelated criteria: First, a true chord, whether consonant or not, is sensitive to mistuning. If any of the tones of such a chord is slightly mistuned, a marked change in the quality of the chord, due to increased roughness, will be perceived. Second, a true chord, though it may include dissonant elements, is formed of a continuous chain or lattice of consonances. The meaning of this statement will become clearer when we examine the spatial representations of the tonal fabrics for the various prime limits in subsequent chapters. It will be seen that combinations of tones that meet these two criteria are likely to correspond to low-numbered harmonic-series segments.

A given type of chord is defined by the collection of odd-number identities it comprises. Consider, for example, the just major triad. In root position and in the most compact voicing, this chord has the relative frequencies 4:5:6. When we analyze this chord in terms of its odd-number identities, however, we discover that it consists of the 1, 5, and 3 identities of the harmonic series. (To find the identities of the tones of any chord, convert the chord to a series of integers, as described above, then factor out any powers of 2 from each of the numbers in the series.) It doesn't matter whether the triad is in root position or in one of its inversions, whether it is in a close or spread voicing, or whether some or all of its tones are duplicated in two or more octaves. As long as there are no additional tones present that do not belong to the triad, every tone must correspond to either a 1, 3, or 5 identity. Thus, all the various series of numbers in Table 3.1 can be taken as representations of the same chord, since all of them can be reduced to some combination of 1, 3, and 5. This, of course, does not mean that all of these various chord voicings sound alike or that they can be freely interchanged without altering the musical effect. It is merely the equivalent of the premise in conventional music theory that every possible combination of the root, third, and fifth of a triad is an instance of that triad.

Just chords may or may not be wholly consonant. Just as there are a finite number of consonant intervals, there are a finite number of chords in which every tone is consonant with every other. We will call chords which meet the preceding condition consonant chords. There are more consonant chords in Just Intonation than are recognized in conventional theory, but they are still relatively few in number. The greater number of possible chords are what I will call, following the example of Ellis, "condissonant chords."[6] These chords include a mixture of consonant and dissonant intervals. I prefer the term "condissonant chord" over the conventional term "dissonant chord" because consonant intervals predominate in such chords and are essential to their comprehensibility. A wholly dissonant chord would be an oxymoron. (Of course, dissonant clusters or aggregates of tones may occur in some styles of music, but it seems a conceptual error to refer to them as chords.) The consonant chords of seven-limit Just Intonation are shown in Table 3.2. The condissonant chords are too numerous to easily classify, but will be discussed in subsequent chapters.

It is also possible to classify chords depending on whether they include a 1 identity (a generator or fundamental). The major triad (1-3-5), the dominant-seventh chord (1-3-5-7), and the dominant-ninth chord (1-3-5-7-9) are examples of chords including a 1 identity. The diminished triad (3-5-7), the minor triad (3-5-15) and the subminor triad (3-7-9) are examples of chords that lack a 1 identity. (The minor triad, when considered from a subharmonic viewpoint, consists of the 1, 3, and 5 identities.) As a general rule, chords which lack a 1 identity can be considered less stable than those which include one.

It is important to avoid confusion between the terms "root" and "fundamental." In this primer, the term "root" has essentially the same meaning that it has in conventional theory: the tone which is in the lowest voice of a chord when the chord is arranged in the order which yields the lowest numbers from a harmonic series point of view. Thus, in the case of the major triad in root position (4:5:6), the root is the tone represented by 4. In the case of the minor triad (10:12:15) the root is the tone represented by 10. The fundamental of a harmonic

Table 3.2: Consonant chords in seven-limit Just Intonation

Name	Relative Frequencies (Root Position)	Odd-Number Identities
Major Triad	4:5:6	1–5–3
Minor Triad	10:12:15	5–3–15
Diminished Triad	5:6:7	5–3–7
Subminor Triad	6:7:9	3–7–9
Dominant-7th Chord	4:5:6:7	1–5–3–7
Dominant-9th Chord	4:5:6:7:9	1–5–3–7–9

series is the tone represented by 1 in the series, and by extension, any other tone that is an octave multiple of the 1 identity (2, 4, 8, 16, …). When a chord has a 1 identity, as in the case of the major triad, the root and the fundamental coincide. When a chord lacks a 1 identity, as in the case of the minor triad, we still refer to the lowest tone of the chord as the root, but the fundamental or 1 identity is absent, although it can be calculated. The fundamental of the minor triad is a tone a 5:4 (10:8) below the root. In the case of a C minor triad, the fundamental would be A♭.

INTERVAL NAMES

Despite the obvious primacy of ratios, it seems neither possible nor desirable to completely avoid the use of conventional interval names, such as "octave," "perfect fifth," "major third," and so forth. These names are familiar to all trained musicians and are intimately associated with specific musical experiences and functions. Although these names are, at present, associated primarily with tempered intervals, where there is an unambiguous relationship between a conventional interval name and a particular just ratio, the two will be treated as synonyms. And when more than one just interval corresponds to a single conventional interval name, qualifying adjectives will be introduced. When an equally tempered interval is meant, it will be clearly indicated, for example, a *tempered* major third, a *tempered* perfect fifth, and so on.

There are a great many more musically useful intervals in Just Intonation than there are in twelve-tone equal temperament, and many of these intervals do not fall neatly into the diatonic scale–derived nomenclature of conventional music theory. A number of theorists, both ancient and modern, have bestowed names on the more common intervals of Just Intonation, resulting in a sometimes bewildering array of terminology. Often, a single interval will have two or three different names in common use, while another, equally important interval will unaccountably have no name whatever except its ratio. The more common interval names will be introduced as circumstances warrant, but the reader should not be overly concerned about grasping or memorizing this obscure nomenclature. The only absolutely reliable form of interval classification in Just Intonation is the ratio, and in this book intervals will never be described by other labels without their ratios being close at hand.

NOTATION

There is no standard system of notation for Just Intonation. The only wholly unambiguous representation of relative pitch in Just Intonation is the ratio, and no composition in Just Intonation ought to be presented to the public in score form without a clear association between whatever symbols are used and the system of ratios relative to whichever tone is designated as $^1/_1$.

Formidable problems confront anyone who attempts to develop a generalized notation for Just Intonation, since it is potentially an open-ended system. The problem, therefore, is one of representing a potentially infinite number of pitches with not merely a finite number, but with a *manageable* number of symbols.

In practice, the lack of a standard notation is less of a problem than one might suspect. If you are working in a fixed scale of twelve or fewer tones per octave, standard staff notation, accompanied by a chart indicating the tunings of the various pitches, will prove adequate. Compositions involving larger tonal sets require different notational solutions. Numerous composers have developed personal notational systems using such devices as different colors, differently shaped note heads, special staves, and flocks of strangely shaped

Table 3.3: Ben Johnston's notation for extended Just Intonation

	Basic Accidentals
♭ / ♯	Raises/lowers by 25:24 (70.7 cents) Difference between 25:16 ($5^4:2^4$) and 24:16 (3:2)
+ / −	Raise/lowers by 81:80 (21.5 cents) Difference between 81:64 ($3^4:2^4$) and 80:64 (5:4)
L / 7	Raises/lowers by 36:35 (48.8 cents) Difference between 36:32 (9:8) and 35:32
↑ / ↓	Raises/lowers by 33:32 (53.3 cents) Difference between 11:8 and 4:3
3 / ε	Raises/lowers by 65:64 (26.8 cents) Difference between 13:8 and 8:5
	Some Compound Accidentals
♯+ / ♭−	Raises/lowers by 135:128 (25:24 + 81:80)
L− / 7+	Raises/lowers by 64:63 (36:35 − 81:80)
♯ / ♭	Raises/lowers by 15:14 (36:35 + 25:24)

accidentals. You will see examples of many such systems in the pages of $^1/_1$ and other periodicals, but none have achieved wide popularity. Since most composers in Just Intonation play their own compositions or are at least directly involved in the rehearsal and performance of their works, this situation has not prevented the composition and performance of significant music. The best-known composer of music in Just Intonation in the twentieth century, Harry Partch, notated his compositions in tablatures that reflected the patterns of the keys or strings of the various instruments he invented. This approach may have made his compositions easier for his players to learn, but the resulting scores are extremely difficult to analyze.

In this publication, I use a set of notational conventions developed by composer Ben Johnston, shown in Table 3.3. This system has many desirable features. It treats the uninflected pitches of Ptolemy's syntonon diatonic in C (the closest thing we have to an "ur-scale" in Just Intonation) as "naturals," uses sharps and flats to represent inflection by a just chromatic semitone (25:24), a usage that is reasonably consistent with conventional notation, and introduces a small number of additional accidentals to represent microtonal inflections resulting from the interaction of various prime factors. Johnston has extended the system through the thirteen limit, but additional symbols could easily be added for higher primes if required. Different accidentals can be combined to represent more complex inflections, as illustrated in Table 3.3. This system works well for compositions that don't venture too far from the home key of C major, but pitches in more remote tonalities can accumulate confusing flocks of accidentals. This is the problem that any generalized system of notation for Just Intonation faces. Novices may have a bit of difficulty in grasping this notation at first, as it presupposes a fairly subtle understanding of Just Intonation. I recommend that you simply accept it as a convention for the moment, then review it as you read the remainder of this publication.

Anomalies

This is an unfortunate term, but since it is already in widespread use, I will not add to the already confusing muddle of intonational terminology by inventing a more agreeable substitute. Anomalies are small discrepancies resulting from sequences of intervals that, in equal temperament, arrive at identical destinations, but that, in Just Intonation, arrive at microtonally distinct pitches.

There are a vast number of such possible intervals, and they have been labeled, usually by ancient or medieval theorists, with a host of confusing names, such as commas, limmas, dieses, skhismas, and so forth. The best known anomalies are the Pythagorean comma, 531,441:524,288 (approximately 23.5 cents), the difference between twelve perfect fifths $(3:2)^{12}$ and seven octaves $(2:1)^7$, and the comma of Didymus or syntonic comma, 81:80 (approximately 21.5 cents), the difference between four perfect fifths $(3:2)^4$ and two octaves plus a major third $(4:1 + 5:4)$. These and other anomalies will be examined in detail in following chapters as we encounter them in our ascent of the ladder of prime numbers.

Many detractors of Just Intonation cite the existence of anomalies as proof that practical music, especially harmonic music, cannot be made in Just Intonation. What is actually demonstrated is that one cannot necessarily use the same compositional techniques in Just Intonation as are used in equal temperament. The important point to recognize is that these so-called anomalies are anomalous only in relation to twelve-tone equal temperament. Twelve-tone equal temperament is a closed system with only twelve unique tones. Every possible melodic or harmonic progression must begin and end on one of these tones. Just Intonation, on the other hand, is best understood as an open system with an unlimited number of unique tones. In this context, a melodic or harmonic progression (provided that it is not played on a fixed-pitch instrument with a limited number of tones) can start or end virtually anywhere. I do not see why the presence of vastly expanded resources should be considered a problem in need of correction, as many of Just Intonation's detractors seem to think. It is, however, important that composers working with Just Intonation be aware of the presence of anomalies and the way they crop up in certain commonly used progressions. Examples of these phenomena will be presented in following chapters.

Tetrachords and Tetrachordal Scales

A tetrachord is a perfect fourth (4:3) which is subdivided into three smaller intervals by means of two intermediate tones. Historically, the tetrachord has served as a basic building block for scales in a number of different cultures. Tetrachordal scales are particularly associated with ancient Greece, the Middle East, and India. The modern Euro-American cultures inherited the concept from the Greeks, by way of Rome. Typically, octave-

Figure 3.4: Disjunct tetrachords

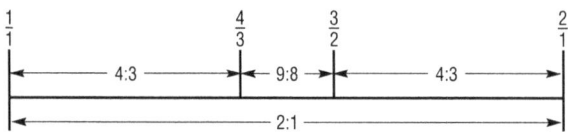

repeating seven-tone scales are created by placing two tetrachords around a central 9:8, as in Figure 3.4. Thus the lower tetrachord begins on $^1/_1$ and the upper one begins on $^3/_2$. Tetrachords arranged this way are said to be *disjunct*. This arrangement is necessary if the scale is to fill an octave. Conjunct tetrachords (where the upper tone of the lower tetrachord and the lower tone of the upper tetrachord are the same) only encompass a minor seventh (16:9) and do not repeat in octaves.

Traditionally, tetrachords and tetrachordal scales are classified according to a system of three *genera* developed by the ancient Greeks. The three classical genera are called the diatonic, the chromatic, and the enharmonic. These three genera (Figure 3.5) are distinguished by a characteristic interval (placed by the Greeks in the highest part of the tetrachord), which remains undivided, while the remainder is divided into two parts. In the case of the enharmonic genus, the characteristic interval is a major third, and the remaining interval of a semitone is divided into two microtones. In the case of the chromatic genus, the characteristic interval is a minor third and the remaining whole tone is divided into two semitones. In the diatonic genus, the characteristic interval is a whole tone, and the remaining minor third is divided in a variety of ways. For each of these three genera, ancient Greek theorists proposed a variety of precise tunings or "shades." Medieval Arabs and Persians discovered many additional possibilities, and modern theorists have added yet more, including some that do not fit neatly to classical genera. We will encounter a variety of tetrachordal scales, some historical and others recently invented, as we explore the properties of the various prime limits in the following chapters. For an exhaustive examination of tetrachords and tetrachordal scales, consult John Chalmers's *Divisions of the Tetrachord*.[7]

There are basically two types of tetrachordal scales: equal-tetrachordal scales, where both tetrachords have the same pattern of intervals, and mixed-tetrachordal scales, where the two tetrachords have different patterns. The Greeks demanded equal-tetrachordal scales, whereas Indian and Arabic/Persian practice allows for scales to be constructed from mixed tetrachords as well.

A further useful property of tetrachords is that six permutations can be created from one basic tetrachord by shifting the positions of the two intermediate tones within the perfect fourth.[8] If we call the three intervals in the tetrachord X, Y, and Z, the six permutations would be (X, Y, Z), (X, Z, Y), (Y, X, Z), (Y, Z, X), (Z, X, Y), and (Z, Y, X). If the different tetrachord permutations are paired to produce new scales, thirty-six possible seven-tone scales can be generated from a single tetrachord.

Figure 3.5: The three tetrachordal genera

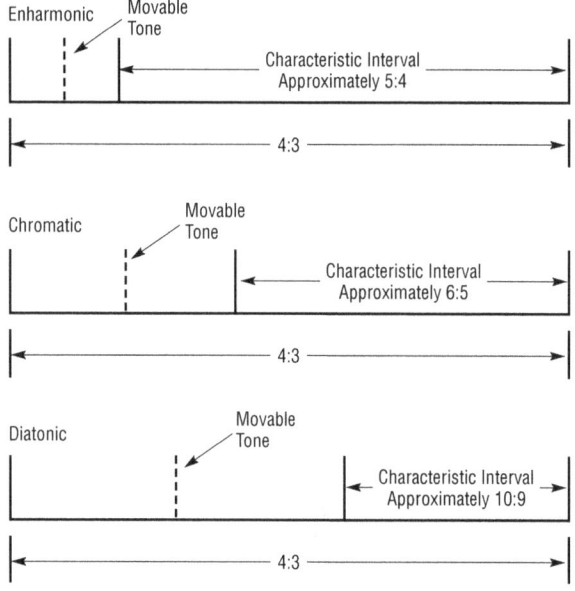

THE LADDER OF PRIMES, PART ONE: TWO, THREE, AND FIVE

As explained in the previous chapters, Just Intonation is based on intervals that can be represented by ratios of relatively small whole numbers. Such intervals can be combined in various ways to create a vast array of scales, modes, and chords. (The nature and importance of whole-number ratios were explained in Chapter Two, "Acoustic and Psychoacoustic Background," and the tools and techniques for manipulating these ratios were presented in Chapter Three, "Basic Definitions, Concepts and Procedures." You should familiarize yourself with the concepts in these chapters before proceeding, and review them if you run into difficulties.)

Twelve-tone equal temperament possesses only twelve unique intervals (admitting octave equivalency), although conventional music theory uses more that twelve names to label them, depending on the contexts in which they occur. Just Intonation, on the other hand, possesses an unlimited number of unique intervals. Of course, not all of these possible intervals are musically significant, but even by a conservative estimate, Just Intonation offers three or four times as many meaningful intervals (not pitches) smaller than an octave as does twelve-tone equal temperament. There are many methods for classifying and organizing the enormous variety of musical resources that Just Intonation provides. Which is most appropriate for your needs will depend on your musical goals and stylistic preferences. However, underlying most theories of Just Intonation is the concept of *prime limits*. We will use this concept to structure this and the following chapter.

In this and the following chapter, we will take a close look at the musical properties of the first four prime numbers, 2, 3, 5, and 7, and briefly examine the primes 11, 13, 17, 19. The properties of 2, 3, and 5 are, for the most part, well documented and understood. Most theorists accept the idea that the scales and chords that form the basis of Western common-practice music theory can be explained in terms of the primes 2, 3, and 5. This does not necessarily mean, however, that conventional common-practice music theory can be applied wholesale to composition in five-limit Just Intonation. Conventional music theory grew up around music that was intended to be performed in some kind of temperament, whether equal, meantone, or well-temperament, and it therefore lacks the necessary tools for dealing with the intervallic subtleties that crop up in five-limit Just Intonation.

The prime number 7 occupies a special position with relation to Western common-practice music. On one hand, certain theorists recognized 7:4 (a flat minor seventh) as a consonance and identified it with the seventh of the dominant-seventh chord (certainly a fundamental constituent of common-practice music) as early as the eighteenth century.[1] On the other hand, by the time theorists began to debate the value of 7, equal temperament, which falsifies the most important 7-based intervals by about one-third of a tempered semitone, was well on its way to becoming entrenched. Thus, while theorists debated whether 7 was consonant and whether it explained the dominant-seventh chord, no one actually *heard* 7-based intervals, at least not in European art music. In American popular music, the situation is rather different. Here, no one debated the significance of ratios, but blues and jazz musicians introduced "blue notes" (flatted thirds, fifths, and sevenths, which hover in the neighborhood of the most consonant 7 ratios) into the national musical vocabulary, and a capella vocal groups, such as barbershop quartets, sang dominant-seventh chords and diminished triads far sweeter than those found on the tempered piano. Thus, 7 has intruded itself to some extent into our musical consciousness, but its implications have been largely ignored by mainstream music theory, which has concerned itself primarily with music composed in Europe between 1700 and 1900. When the properties of the intervals spawned by 7 are examined in detail, it will be seen that they can add to the vocabulary of Western tonal music a host of surprising new melodic and harmonic possibilities. Primes above 7 (11, 13, 17, 19, ...) have been used to good effect by a limited number of composers, but they are, with the possible exception of 17 in the context of the diminished-seventh chord, foreign to Western music both in theory and in practice.

ONE, THE FOUNDATION

Before we start our climb up the ladder, we will pause for a moment to examine the ground on which we are standing. At the root of any possible system of Just Intonation, we find the number 1. The number 1 is not considered prime, being an essential constituent of the definition of primeness, but 1 is nevertheless the starting point for the generation of any just tuning system. Normally expressed as the ratio $^1/_1$, 1 represents the fixed point to which the relative frequencies of other tones are compared. What absolute frequency $^1/_1$ is assigned is strictly a matter of personal preference or convenience. Just Intonation is not concerned with absolute pitch, but only with precise *relative* pitch. In the examples in this publication we will identify $^1/_1$ with the note C, for the sake of simplicity. As an interval, 1:1 represents the unison, the "noninterval" between two tones with exactly the same frequency.

TWO, THE EMPTY MATRIX

The first musically important prime, 2, generates the octave, 2:1 (1200 cents). 2:1 is the *primary interval* based on 2. 2:1 is the only interval Just Intonation and equal temperament have in common. Multiply the frequency of any tone by 2, and the result will be the tone one octave higher. Divide the frequency of any tone by 2, and you'll get the tone one octave lower. The same thing is true for any power of 2. Multiplying or dividing a frequency by four yields a tone two octaves higher or lower; multiplying or dividing a frequency by eight yields a tone three octaves higher or lower; and so on. While most of us would agree that the octave is a musically necessary interval, we could not do much with a musical system consisting only of octaves of a single tone. The octave is simply the empty frame which must by filled with additional tones to make a useful scale. To generate those additional tones, we require the services of other primes.

THE THREE LIMIT (PYTHAGOREAN TUNING)

The next prime number is 3. The primary interval for 3 is the just perfect fifth, 3:2 (701.96 cents). 3:2 is the first of many intervals we will encounter that can generate tones with which to fill the empty octaves generated by the prime number 2. If we tune a 3:2 upward from C ($^1/_1$) we generate a new pitch, G ($^3/_2$). In so doing, we imply an additional interval, that between G ($^3/_2$) and the C ($^2/_1$) above. This interval is 4:3, the just perfect fourth (498.04 cents). 3:2 and 4:3 are *complements*. If we tune a 3:2 below C' ($^2/_1$) or a 4:3 above $^1/_1$, we generate another new tone, F ($^4/_3$). By chaining additional 3:2s and/or 4:3s, we can generate any number of unique tones. Scales generated using only 2:1, 3:2, and 4:3 are known as *three-limit* scales, meaning that they involve no prime factor greater than 3. Scales of this type are also known as *Pythagorean* scales, after Pythagoras of Samos, the Greek philosopher/mathematician who is credited with their introduction to the Greek-speaking world. They are the oldest known just scales, having been described in Babylonian clay tablets from the second millennium B.C.E. They are also the easiest scales to tune by ear.

THE PYTHAGOREAN (DITONE) DIATONIC SCALE

The method for generating a major diatonic scale from 3:2s and 4:3s is illustrated in Figure 4.1. The resulting scale degrees are $^1/_1$, $^9/_8$, $^{81}/_{64}$, $^4/_3$, $^3/_2$, $^{27}/_{16}$, and $^{243}/_{128}$. This is known as a Pythagorean diatonic scale. It is also sometimes called the *ditone* diatonic, after its characteristic major third (81:64), which is called a ditone because it is the sum of two whole tones (9:8 + 9:8). All of the intervals smaller than 2:1 in the ditone diatonic are shown in Figure 4.2. To find the interval between two tones

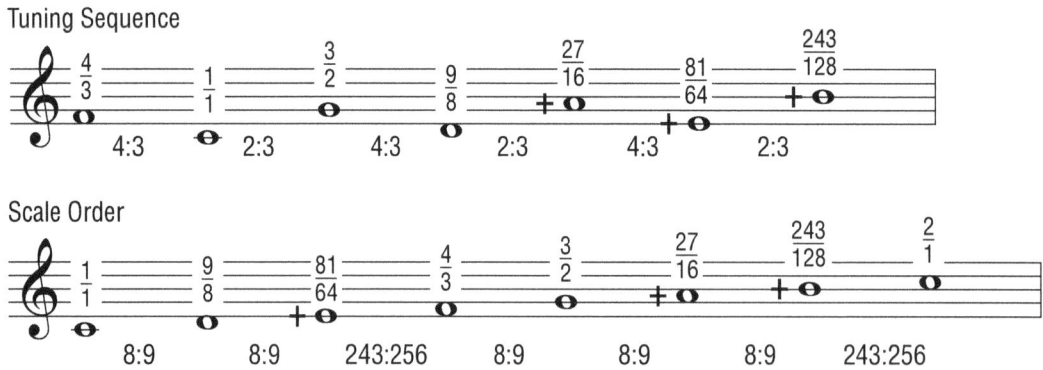

Figure 4.1: Pythagorean diatonic tuning

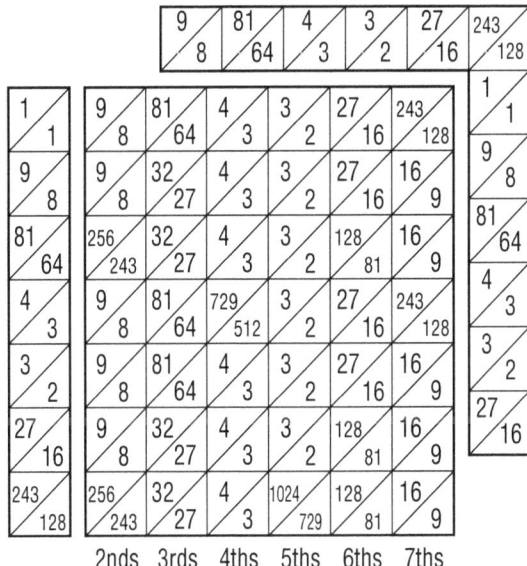

Figure 4.2: All of the intervals less than 2:1 in the Pythagorean diatonic scale

using this chart, find the ratio of the lower tone in the vertical column to the left of the square. Read to the right along the horizontal row to the right of the ratio until that row intersects the diagonal leading to the ratio representing the higher tone in the upside-down L-shaped figure to the upper right of the square. For example, to find the interval between E+ $^{81}/_{64}$ and B+ $^{243}/_{128}$, find $^{81}/_{64}$ in the left-hand column, then follow the diagonal from $^{243}/_{128}$ in the L-shaped figure until it intersects the row to the right of $^{81}/_{64}$. The answer is 3:2. The ditone diatonic is an *equal-tetrachordal* scale, the first of many such historical scales we will encounter in our exploration of expanding prime limits. The tetrachords of the ditone diatonic are divided into two 9:8 whole tones and one 256:243 semitone or Pythagorean *limma*.

The Pythagorean diatonic scale is clearly a form of Just Intonation, since it is generated using only the simple whole-number ratios 2:1, 3:2, and 4:3. However, Pythagorean tuning is somewhat at odds with the preference for the simplest ratios compatible with a given musical purpose. Its fourths and fifths are all 4:3s and 3:2s, which are clearly the simplest ratios available for those intervals, but its thirds and sixths are complex intervals such as 32:27, 81:64, 27:16, and 128:81. Western music theory and practice treats the thirds and sixths as important consonances, surpassed only by the fourth, fifth, and octave, but the thirds and sixths of the Pythagorean scale are tense, dissonant intervals, as their ratios indicate. As we will demonstrate shortly, more consonant thirds and sixths can be generated using the next prime number, 5. The most consonant intervals available in a Pythagorean tuning, after the octave, fourth, and fifth, are the major second (9:8), its extension, the major ninth (9:4), and its complement, the minor seventh (16:9).

Pythagorean Chromatic Scales and the Pythagorean Comma

The Pythagorean tuning method used above is not limited to seven-tone scales. The process of chaining 3:2s can be continued indefinitely, without ever producing an octave duplicate of the starting tone. Figure 4.3 illustrates the tones generated by tuning six 3:2s up and six 3:2s down from $^1/_1$, for a total of thirteen tones. Musicians trained in conventional music theory will be familiar with the "circle of fifths." Examining the figure, we see that just perfect fifths do not form a closed circle. The two tones at the extreme limits of the chain of 3:2s, G♭-- ($^{1024}/_{729}$) and F♯++ ($^{729}/_{512}$), are not the same. The difference between these two tones is the small interval 531,441:524,288 (approximately 23.5 cents), known as the Pythagorean comma. In slightly different terms, the sum of twelve 3:2s ($3^{12}:2^{12}$) is greater than seven octaves ($2^7:1$) by a Pythagorean comma. The Pythagorean comma is the first of several intonational *anomalies* we will encounter. In twelve-tone equal temperament this difference is distributed among the twelve perfect fifths, each fifth being flatted by $^1/_{12}$ of a Pythagorean comma (approximately 1.96 cents), thereby causing the twelve fifths to form a closed circle. In fact, twelve-tone equal temperament can be considered a fair approximation of Pythagorean tuning. At least it is much better for this purpose than for representing five-limit Just Intonation, the purpose for which, unfortunately, it is normally used.

Figure 4.3: The Pythagorean comma

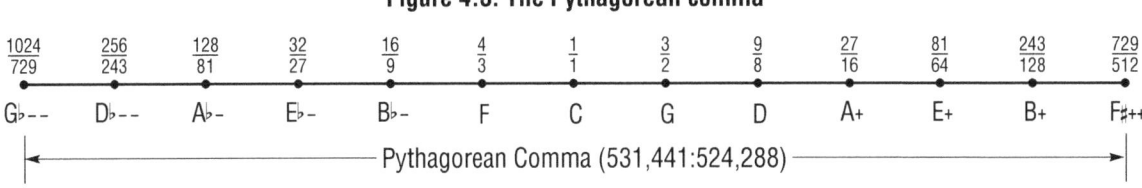

The Ladder of Primes: Part One

A first encounter with the Pythagorean comma may lead the unwary reader to a serious misunderstanding, which is usually expressed in a question like the following: "You mean if I have properly tuned fifths and fourths, I can't have properly tuned octaves?" The answer to this question is a loud and unequivocal NO! Octaves are octaves and fifths are fifths, and neither is derived from the other. In more formal terms, no integer power of any prime number m is equal to any integer power of any other prime number n. Octaves are powers of 2 and perfect fifths are powers of 3. No number of one will ever equal any number of the other. This fact in no way interferes with having both coexist in a practical tuning system.[2]

Chords

Given its lack of consonant intervals, it should come as no surprise that the three limit is not very well equipped when it comes to chords. The Pythagorean major and minor triads have the relative frequencies 64: 81:96 and 54:64:81, respectively — certainly beyond the limits of the definition of a chord in the "Basic Definitions" chapter as a series of low-number identities of a harmonic series. They fail the other criteria for a chord as well, because the Pythagorean thirds are not particularly sensitive to mistuning. The Pythagorean thirds generate beats, as described previously, and mistuning them slightly only causes the beats to become a little faster or slower. Since the Pythagorean thirds are not consonances, neither the major nor the minor triad in Pythagorean tuning is a continuous chain of consonant intervals.

Given the unsuitability of the Pythagorean triads, about the only acceptable chords in the three limit are the so-called "open triad" of root, perfect fifth, and octave (2:3:4),[3] which serves as the final chord for most medieval and Renaissance polyphonic compositions, and the comparatively discordant combinations 4:6:9 and 9:12:16, which result from the stacking of two 3:2s or two 4:3s respectively. The latter two are really the same chord, consisting of the identities 1, 3, and 9, but in two different inversions and voicings. In the close voicing 6:8:9, conventional music theory would label this as a suspended-fourth chord. It also provides the framework for La Monte Young's "Dream Chords," in which a fourth tone from a higher prime limit is added to subdivide the 9:8 interval. One could create larger chords from chains of consecutive 3:2s or 4:3s, but the number of such intervals that can be stacked before dissonance becomes the predominant factor is relatively small.

Although three-limit scales are poorly suited to chordal harmony, they work well melodically and are eminently suitable for polyphony based on fourths and fifths, such as the motets and organa of the European Ars Antiqua period (c. 1100–1300 C.E.). Pythagorean scales were the sole theoretical basis for intonation throughout the European Middle Ages. The compositional practices of this period, which treat thirds and sixths as dissonances, are understandable in light of the properties of Pythagorean tuning.

Three-limit scales are more important for their historical and ethnomusicological interest than as resources for the composition of new music. The lack of consonant intervals and chords within this prime limit make it nearly useless as a source of expanded tonal resources. Nonetheless, the perfect consonances of the three limit, 3:2, and 4:3, are essential constituents of chords involving intervals from higher prime limits, and in conjunction with 9:8 they from the framework for all tetrachordal scales.

The ability of the Pythagorean series to generate an unlimited number of unique tones has had a powerful and not always salutary effect on musical thinking in both Eastern and Western cultures. Many theorists across the centuries have insisted that all musical intervals can or should be derived from a series or "cycle" of fifths. Although it is true that if the Pythagorean series is extended far enough it will include various close approximations to simple intervals derived from other primes, it is much simpler to generate consonances involving other primes directly, rather than attempting to approximate them with long chains of 3:2s. As will be demonstrated in the next chapter, a multidimensional system of Just Intonation, generated by several primes, provides a much greater variety of tonal resources with a smaller number of tones than can any comparable extension of the Pythagorean series.

The Five Limit

As stated previously, in order to generate consonant thirds and sixths, we require the next prime number, 5. The primary interval for 5 is 5:4, the just major third (386.3 cents). This interval is the serene consonance we expect a major third to be. It is narrower than the Pythagorean ditone, 81:64, by 81:80, approximately 21.5 cents. This interval, known as the comma of Didymus or the syntonic comma, is the most important anomaly in the five limit. Expressed differently, the syntonic comma is the difference between four perfect fifths less two octaves ($3^4 \times 2^{-2}$) and 5:4. The importance of this interval will be revealed presently.

Subtracting a 5:4 from the just perfect fifth, 3:2, yields 6:5, the just minor third (315.6 cents). In other words, the simplest possible division of the perfect fifth yields the major and minor thirds. Complementing these two intervals yields the just minor sixth, 8:5 (813.7 cents) and the just major sixth, 5:3 (884.4 cents), respectively. These four intervals are the principal consonances of the five limit. We now have the materials we need to construct just major and minor triads. The just major triad in root position consists of three tones with the relative frequencies 4:5:6. In other words, the major triad consists of a major third (5:4) below and a minor third (6:5) above. The outer interval is, of course, a perfect fifth (6:4 = 3:2). The minor triad has the relative frequencies 10:12:15. That is, it consists of a minor third (12:10 = 6:5) below and a major third (15:12 = 5:4) above, the outer interval being, again, a perfect fifth (15:10 = 3:2). Thus, both the major and minor triads are products of the five limit. We will make a detailed examination of the major and minor triads and other chords native to the five limit later in this chapter. For the moment, however, we will take their existence for granted and turn our attention to their role in scale construction.

Constructing a Five-Limit Major Scale

It is traditional to construct a just major scale from three interlocking major triads, built on the tonic ($^1/_1$), dominant ($^3/_2$), and subdominant ($^4/_3$) scale degrees. An analogous procedure can be used to generate a natural-minor (Aeolian) scale from three minor triads. As experienced Just Intonation users know, and as we will demonstrate shortly, this method of scale construction creates problems that are at the crux of the long-standing debate over the practicality of Just Intonation for harmonic music. Nevertheless, we will proceed with the traditional method and then examine the problems it creates.

The procedure for tuning the just major scale is illustrated in Figure 4.4. We begin by tuning a major triad on the tonic ($^1/_1$). This gives us the scale degrees $^1/_1$, $^5/_4$, and $^3/_2$. Next, we construct another major triad on the dominant degree, the fifth of the previous triad ($^3/_2$). This yields two additional tones, $^9/_8$ and $^{15}/_8$. Finally, we obtain the subdominant degree ($^4/_3$) by tuning a fifth below (or a fourth above) $^1/_1$, and then construct our last triad on this tone. This process gives us our final two scale tones, $^4/_3$ and $^5/_3$. Expressed in scale order, starting on the tonic, the scale degrees are $^1/_1$, $^9/_8$, $^5/_4$, $^4/_3$, $^3/_2$, $^5/_3$, and $^{15}/_8$.

This scale is nearly 2000 years old. It is described in the *Harmonics* of the second century C.E. Greco-Roman theorist Claudius Ptolemy, and is known as the *syntonon*

Figure 4.4: Ptolemy's syntonon diatonic tuning

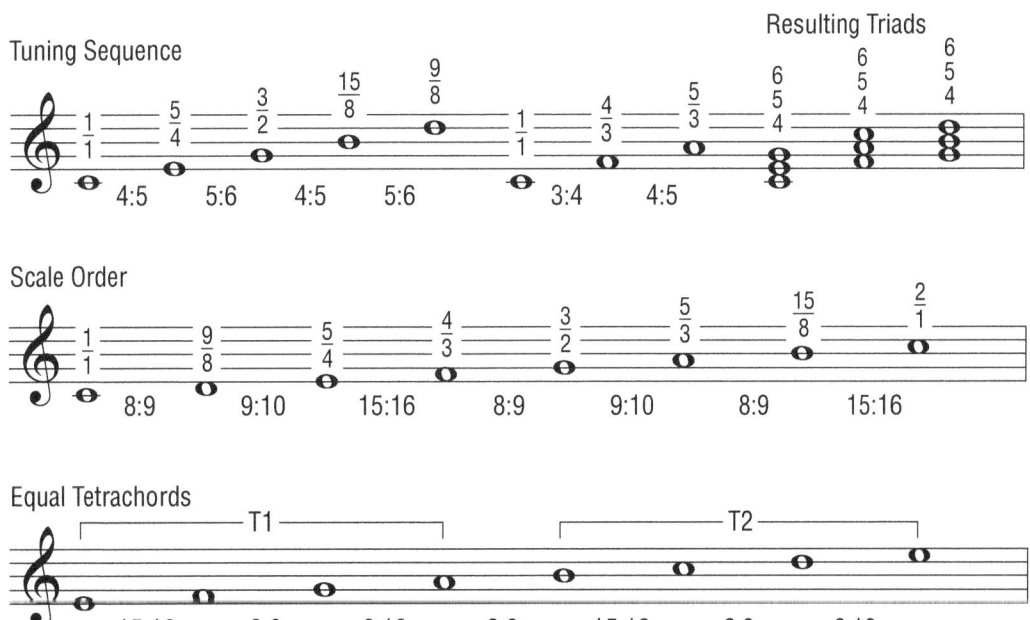

(intense, severe, or tightly stretched) diatonic.[4] Like the Pythagorean diatonic scale, the syntonon diatonic is tetrachordal. Viewed as an octave scale starting on C, the tetrachords are not equal, however. The lower tetrachord has the form 1 <8:9> 2 <9:10> 3 <15:16> 4, whereas the upper tetrachord has the 9:8 and 10:9 reversed. However, if we take E ($5/4$) as the starting tone (as the Greeks did), we find that the scale is in fact composed of two equal, disjunct tetrachords of the pattern 1 <15:16> 2♭ <8:9> 3 <9:10> 4.

Whereas Pythagorean scales are one dimensional, being generated by chaining a single interval, the syntonon diatonic is two dimensional, being the product of two unique intervals, the perfect fifth (3:2) and the major third (5:4). In Figure 4.5, the syntonon diatonic is represented by a two-dimensional lattice. Each horizontal line segment in the chart represents a perfect fifth (3:2) or a perfect fourth (4:3). Each vertical line segment represents a major third (5:4) or a minor sixth (8:5). Octaves are not represented in this chart; each ratio should be thought of as representing the occurrence of that particular tone in all possible octaves. A major triad is represented as two line segments joined at a right angle, with the opening facing the upper right. A minor triad is represented as a right angle open to the lower left.

Figure 4.6 shows all of the possible intervals smaller than 2:1 in the syntonon diatonic. Contrast this with the chart of all of the intervals in the ditone diatonic (Figure 4.2). All of the 81:64s and 128:81s have been replaced by consonant 5:4s and 8:5s, and, in all but one case, 32:27s and 27:16s have been replaced by consonant 6:5s and 5:3s. The two Pythagorean semitones or *limmas* (256:243s) have been replaced by the much simpler just diatonic semitone, 16:15 (111.7 cents). The Pythagorean major seventh, 243:128, has been replaced by the just diatonic major seventh, 15:8 (1088.3 cents). In addition, there is a second variety of major second, 10:9 (182.4 cents), known variously as the small whole step or minor tone, and its complement, the acute minor seventh, 9:5

Figure 4.5: Ptolemy's syntonon diatonic as a two-dimensional lattice

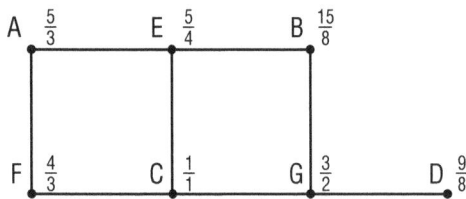

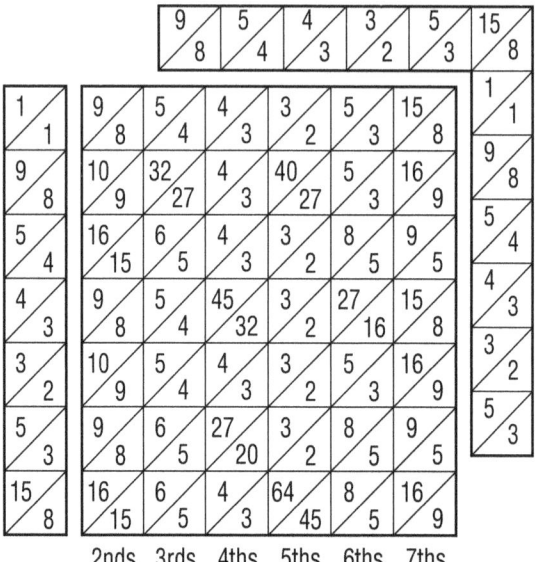

Figure 4.6: All of the intervals less than 2:1 in Ptolemy's syntonon diatonic

(1017.6 cents). For reasons that are unclear to me, critics of Just Intonation often cite the existence of two different whole tones in the diatonic scale, 9:8 and 10:9, as evidence that Just Intonation is impractical. 9:8 and 10:9 represent the simplest possible division of 5:4 into two parts. Thus, these two intervals have the same relation to the major third as the major and minor thirds have to the perfect fifth. I suppose the critics consider anything that is unlike equal temperament to be a problem. I have yet to see any of them propose that the perfect fifth be divided into two equal, neutral thirds, which would be a logical extension of their attitude toward the major third and the whole tones.

THE SUPERTONIC PROBLEM

As great an improvement as the syntonon diatonic represents over the ditone model from a harmonic point of view, it is, as stated previously, not without problems of its own. In examining the columns of fourths and fifths in Figure 4.6, you may have observed that the syntonon diatonic has one 3:2 and one 4:3 fewer than the ditone diatonic. Specifically, the relationship between D $9/8$ and A $5/3$ is 40:27, the grave, imperfect, or "wolf" fifth (680.4 cents), rather than the desired 3:2. The complement of this relationship is 27:20, the acute or imperfect fourth (519.6 cents). As one would expect, these are dissonant intervals, quite unlikely to be mistaken for the perfect fifth and fourth. The wolf fifth is present in the syntonon diatonic because A $5/3$ was tuned as the

Figure 4.7:
The syntonon diatonic and the syntonic comma

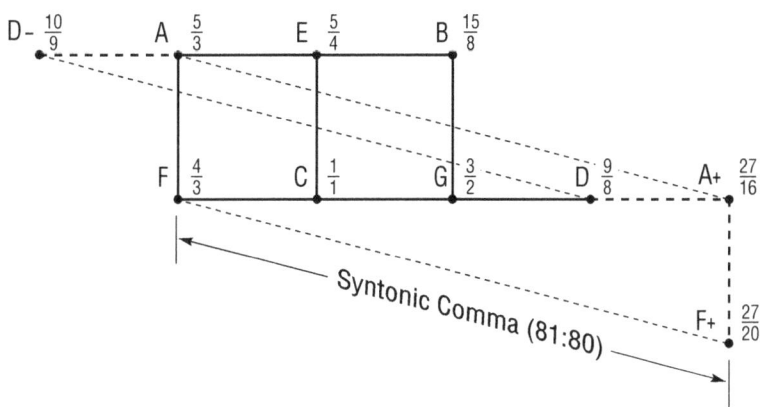

major third of the subdominant (F $4/3$), whereas D $9/8$ was tuned as the perfect fifth of the dominant (G $3/2$). The perfect fifth of D $9/8$ is A+ $27/16$, the sixth degree of the ditone diatonic. In other words, the perfect fifth of D $9/8$ and the major third of F $4/3$ are two distinct tones, which differ by 81:80, the syntonic comma. We have already encountered this interval as the difference between the mistuned harmonics of the Pythagorean ditone or the difference between the ditone (81:64) and the just major third (5:4). The syntonic comma is also the interval by which the imperfect fifth, 40:27, is narrower than 3:2, and by which the imperfect fourth is wider than 4:3. In addition to forming an imperfect fifth with A $5/3$, D $9/8$ forms a Pythagorean minor third (32:27) with F $4/3$, the only such interval in the scale. As a result, the minor triad on D has the relative frequencies 27:32:40. In contrast, the other two minor triads in the syntonon diatonic, on E $5/4$ and A $5/3$, have the desired relative frequencies 10:12:15. The bad minor triad on D (the supertonic) has been the bane of composers and theorists working with five-limit Just Intonation for the last 400 years.

To correct the intonation of the supertonic minor triad, one or more of its tones must be adjusted by a syntonic comma. Since F $4/3$ and A $5/3$ already form a 5:4, the simplest solution is to lower D $9/8$ by a syntonic comma to D- $10/9$, thereby correcting the intonation of both the fifth and the minor third. This results in a scale with three good minor triads, but only two good major triads, the major triad on G now having the imperfect fifth (10:9 × 2:3 = 40:27). It is, in fact, the relative minor of the syntonon diatonic, and is the same scale that would be generated by tuning three minor triads with the relative frequencies 10:12:15 on A $5/3$, D- $10/9$, and E $5/4$. It can also be viewed as the complement of the major scale, transposed by 8:5 (see Figure 4.8). Thus, we have created a new scale that is just as useful as the one we started with, but we have not solved the problem of the bad triad, we have merely moved it to a different position in the scale.

The alternative is to retain D $9/8$ and raise F $4/3$ *and* A $5/3$ by a syntonic comma to F+ $27/20$ and A+ $27/16$, to produce a good minor triad on that tone. This solution produces considerably worse results. It introduces two wolves, between F+ $27/20$ and C $1/1$ (between the subdominant and the tonic) and between A+ $27/16$ and E $5/4$, thereby mistuning both the major triad on the fourth degree and the minor triad on the sixth (Figure 4.9). You can try various strategies for solving this problem, but several hundred years of tuning experience show that you will only succeed in moving the bad triad from one scale degree to another. You will never create something

Figure 4.8: A five-limit minor scale generated by three minor triads

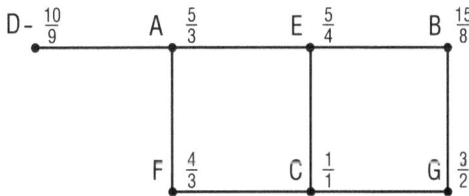

Figure 4.9: The syntonon diatonic with an added minor triad on D $9/8$

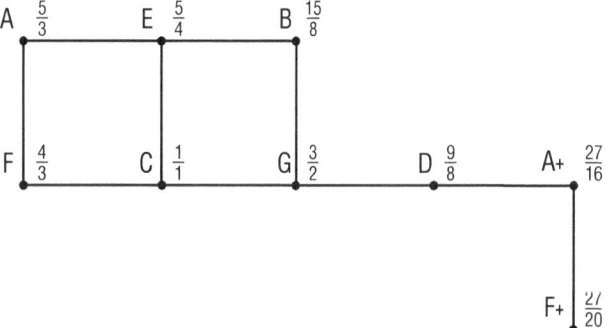

resembling a diatonic scale with only seven tones and six good triads.[5]

The problems posed by the supertonic minor triad and the syntonic comma have provoked some rather extreme reactions from composers and theorists. These phenomena have led many conventionally minded theorists to condemn Just Intonation as impractical for harmonic music, and conversely they have caused some of the most staunch defenders of Just Intonation to condemn the idea of scales as foreign to just tunings. I consider both of these positions to be in error. Harmonic music in Just Intonation is both possible and practical, not to mention extremely beautiful. However, successful harmonic music in Just Intonation does not slavishly follow the conventions of common-practice harmony, which were established under the influence of meantone and equally tempered tunings. Harmonic music in Just Intonation must obey its own natural laws; it often requires sets of tones that exceed the bounds of fixed diatonic or chromatic scales.

On the other hand, fixed scales, usually of five or seven tones-per-octave, are an important part of our musical heritage and are a fascinating study in their own right. They are the wellspring of melodic art, and ought not to be neglected or discarded simply because they sometimes conflict with that recent innovation, triadic harmony. We have inherited a rich store of just scales from a variety of sophisticated musical cultures, especially ancient Greece and classical Islam. Each of these scales is a valuable resource with a unique mood, and with important lessons to teach about the effect of just intervals in varying combinations. Whether one uses these scales strictly, or in combination with additional tones for harmonic support and elaboration, they are a valuable resource which no serious student of Just Intonation should ignore.

One can use Just Intonation to create music in a great variety of styles. At one extreme is pure, unaccompanied melody. At the opposite extreme is music in which harmonic progression is the dominant organizing principle, and melody is subordinate or even absent. Between these extremes are an infinite range of possibilities: melody with a drone, heterophony or simultaneous variation, accompanied melody in which harmonic support is subordinate to the melodic line, accompanied melody which grows out of harmonic progressions, and numerous types of polyphony, which may or may not be based on a harmonic foundation. Each of these styles will require different intonational resources. Some compositions will require only a handful of unique tones, while others may require dozens (or in extreme cases, hundreds). It is, therefore, useless to generalize about what kinds of tonal sets are required for composition in Just Intonation, much less to try to create any kind of "ultimate tuning system" to serve the needs of future generations. What is necessary is to understand the principles of harmonic and melodic connection in Just Intonation. Thus equipped, you will be able to select appropriate intonational resources for each compositional task.

THE FIVE-LIMIT LATTICE

We explained earlier that a series of 3:2s or 4:3s could be extended indefinitely without ever reaching any tone that is an exact octave duplicate of any other tone in the series. This same condition applies to the other primary interval of the five limit, 5:4 (or to its complement, 8:5). That is, a series of 5:4s or 8:5s can also be extended indefinitely without ever reaching any tone that is an octave duplicate of any other tone in the series. Further, a series of 5:4s and a series of 3:2s can have only one common tone or point of intersection. This allows us to visualize five-limit Just Intonation as a two-dimensional lattice, in which one dimension is defined by 3:2 (or 4:3) and the other dimension is defined by 5:4 (or 8:5).

Figure 4.10 illustrates a finite region of this lattice nine columns of 5:4s wide and five rows of 3:2s high, centered on C $^1/_1$. Again, as in the graphic representation of the syntonon diatonic, each horizontal link in the lattice represents a 3:2 or 4:3, and each vertical link represents a 5:4 or 8:5. The prime number 2 is not represented in this chart. Each ratio represents the occurrence of that tone in all possible octaves. As a result, the distinction between complementary intervals is not represented. For instance, the horizontal link between $^1/_1$ and $^4/_3$ represents both the interval between $^1/_1$ and the $^4/_3$ *above* it, that is, a 4:3, and the interval between $^1/_1$ and the $^4/_3$ below it, that is, a 3:2.

The type of chart in Figure 4.10, which will be used throughout this primer, makes intervallic relationships explicit. In general, the closer two tones are in the lattice, the simpler their relationship. Any two tones in the lattice that are in the same spatial relationship are connected by the same interval. Thus, although the tones at the corners of the chart are related to $^1/_1$ by very complex intervals, they are connected to their nearest neighbors by the same simple intervals that connect the tones in the vicinity of $^1/_1$.

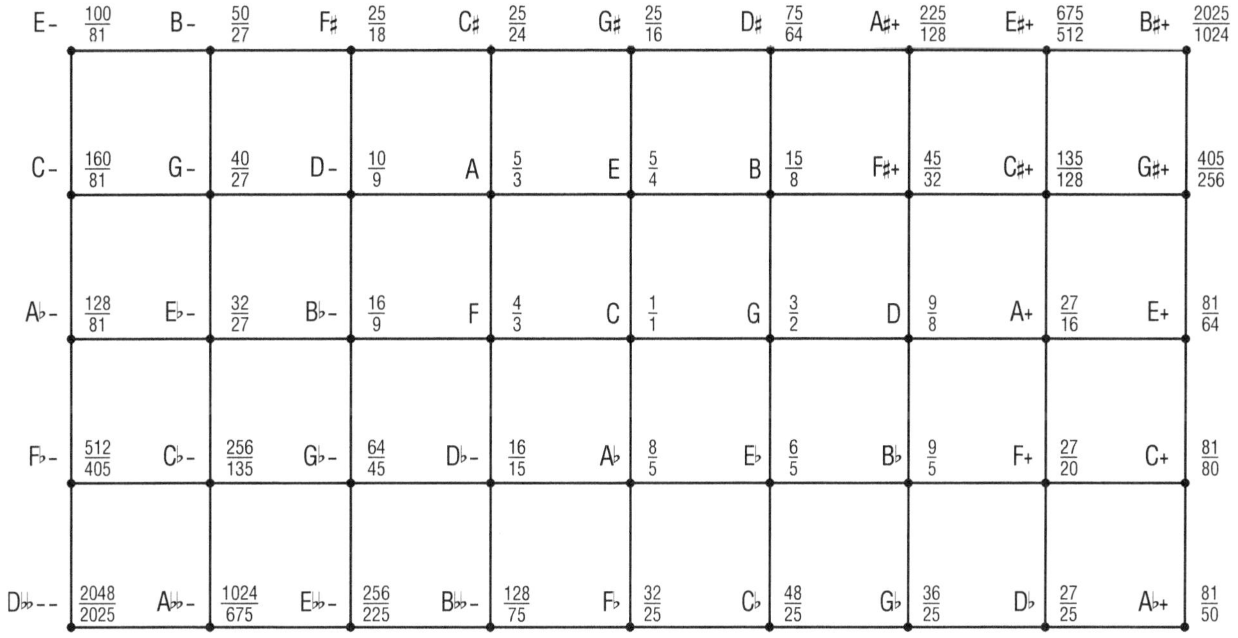

E- $\frac{100}{81}$	B- $\frac{50}{27}$	F♯ $\frac{25}{18}$	C♯ $\frac{25}{24}$	G♯ $\frac{25}{16}$	D♯ $\frac{75}{64}$	A♯+ $\frac{225}{128}$	E♯+ $\frac{675}{512}$	B♯+ $\frac{2025}{1024}$		
C- $\frac{160}{81}$	G- $\frac{40}{27}$	D- $\frac{10}{9}$	A $\frac{5}{3}$	E $\frac{5}{4}$	B $\frac{15}{8}$	F♯+ $\frac{45}{32}$	C♯+ $\frac{135}{128}$	G♯+ $\frac{405}{256}$		
A♭- $\frac{128}{81}$	E♭- $\frac{32}{27}$	B♭- $\frac{16}{9}$	F $\frac{4}{3}$	C $\frac{1}{1}$	G $\frac{3}{2}$	D $\frac{9}{8}$	A+ $\frac{27}{16}$	E+ $\frac{81}{64}$		
F♭- $\frac{512}{405}$	C♭- $\frac{256}{135}$	G♭- $\frac{64}{45}$	D♭- $\frac{16}{15}$	A♭ $\frac{8}{5}$	E♭ $\frac{6}{5}$	B♭ $\frac{9}{5}$	F+ $\frac{27}{20}$	C+ $\frac{81}{80}$		
D♭♭-- $\frac{2048}{2025}$	A♭♭- $\frac{1024}{675}$	E♭♭- $\frac{256}{225}$	B♭♭- $\frac{128}{75}$	F♭ $\frac{32}{25}$	C♭ $\frac{48}{25}$	G♭ $\frac{36}{25}$	D♭ $\frac{27}{25}$	A♭+ $\frac{81}{50}$		

Figure 4.10: A portion of the five-limit lattice

Adriaan Fokker invented an elegant way of representing any interval in the five-limit fabric by a pair of integers indicating the number of links on the two axes of the lattice. The first number of the pair represents links on the horizontal (3:2) axis, and the second represents links on the vertical (5:4) axis. Positive values represent movement upward or to the right, and negative values represent movement downward or to the left. Thus, a perfect fifth is (1, 0) and a perfect fourth is (−1, 0); a major third is (0, 1) and a minor sixth is (0, −1).

It is easy to determine the interval between any two tones in the lattice by comparing that relationship to an analogous relationship involving $^1/_1$. In other words, we ask the question, "what tone is related to $^1/_1$ as a is related to b?" Suppose, for instance, we wanted to know the interval between D $^9/_8$ and C+ $^{81}/_{80}$. On the lattice, the relationship between D $^9/_8$ and C+ $^{81}/_{80}$ is (2, −1). The tone with the same relationship to $^1/_1$ is B♭ $^9/_5$. Therefore, C+ $^{81}/_{80}$ is a 9:5 above D $^9/_8$. Conversely, the relationship between C+ $^{81}/_{80}$ and D $^9/_8$ is (−2, 1). Taking this route from $^1/_1$, we arrive at D- $^{10}/_9$. Therefore, D $^9/_8$ is a 10:9 above C+ $^{81}/_{80}$. 9:5 and 10:9 are, of course, complements, and this reveals another useful property of the lattice, namely that two tones that are related to a third tone by complementary intervals are located at equal distances in opposite directions from that tone (and that an interval can be complemented by negating the numbers representing its position on the lattice). This is most obvious in the case of $^1/_1$, because the ratios that label the other tones make their relationships with $^1/_1$ explicit. The whole lattice can be viewed as a set of complementary pairs of tones arrayed symmetrically around $^1/_1$. However, the same is true of every tone on the lattice. The facts that the portion of the lattice illustrated in Figure 4.10 is symmetrical around $^1/_1$ and that $^1/_1$ is assigned the Western pitch name "C" are essentially arbitrary conventions. The lattice is really infinite and therefore has no center. Thus there is no implicit hierarchy among the tones of the lattice. (Hierarchies may be implicit in the limited sets of tones chosen for specific compositions, or they may be established by the ways tones are introduced, departed from, approached, and combined.) Any point on the lattice can become $^1/_1$, and $^1/_1$ can be assigned any practical frequency and given whatever name one chooses (or none at all).

Just as every unique interval on the lattice is represented by a characteristic spatial relationship, every possible type of scale, chord, or other tonal formation can be represented by a characteristic geometric figure. We have already encountered one such figure in the representation of the syntonon diatonic in Figure 4.5. Hereafter, whenever new scales, chords, or other tonal relationships are introduced, they will be represented by their characteristic geometric figures. It is easy to determine what tones are required for the transposition of any scale or chord by means of the lattice. One

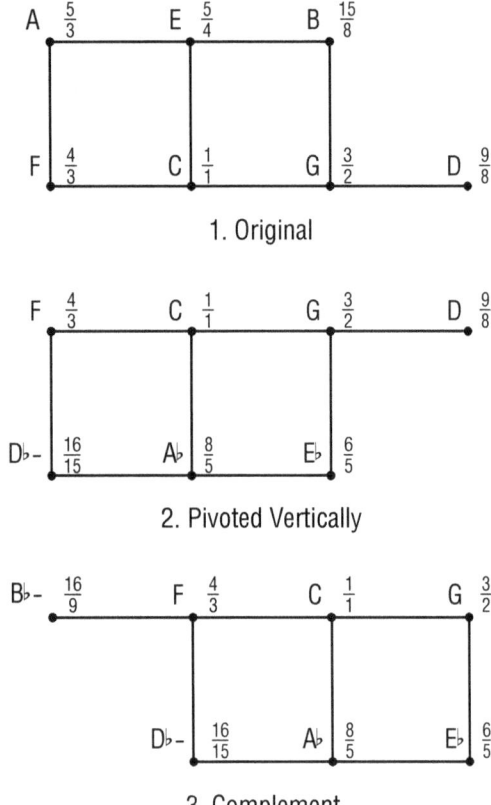

Figure 4.11: Complementing the syntonon diatonic

simply moves the characteristic figure on the lattice so that some new tone occupies the position formerly occupied by the root or tonic. For instance, if we wished to transpose the syntonon diatonic from the key of C $^1/_1$ to the key of D♭- $^{16}/_{15}$, we would simply shift the figure down by one link and to the left by one link, placing $^{16}/_{15}$ in the position formerly occupied by $^1/_1$. The lattice can also show the results of complementing chords and scales. This involves rotating the characteristic figure on both its horizontal and vertical axes, using the tonic as a pivot. This may be a bit difficult to visualize, so we'll illustrate the process in Figure 4.11. Here, the syntonon diatonic on C $^1/_1$ is complemented to form a natural minor scale on F $^4/_3$. The figure is rotated on both of its axes, using $^1/_1$ as a pivot. The two scales share the same set of intervals between scale degrees, but their order is reversed. It is recommended that you make several copies of the five-limit lattice and use them for mapping scales, chords, harmonic progressions, and so forth, as you proceed through this publication. The author has found this to be an extremely useful technique for understanding extended Just Intonation.

The extended tonal fabric provided by the five-limit lattice can be understood in many ways. It can be viewed as a lattice of interlocking major and minor triads, as a matrix in which fixed scales can be transposed, or as a field of intervals through which melodies and harmonic progressions can roam freely, unconstrained by the twelve-tone "squirrel cage." All of these views are equally correct. Which one takes precedence depends on your musical preferences.

Although no tone in the five-limit lattice is an exact duplicate of any other, there are many pairs of tones which differ by very small intervals. We have already encountered two of these so-called "anomalies," the Pythagorean comma (531,441:524,288) and the syntonic comma, 81:80. In terms of position on the lattice, these intervals are respectively (12, 0) and (4, −1). In addition to these, there are many more small inequalities in the five-limit fabric. In fact, if the fabric is extended infinitely an infinite number of inequalities will be found, but most involve tones too remote from one another to be of musical significance. There is, however, at least one remaining anomaly in the five-limit fabric that has obvious musical significance.

THE GREAT DIESIS

The great or enharmonic diesis (ratio 128:125, approximately 41.1 cents) is the interval between two tones separated by three vertical links (0, −3) on the lattice. In other words, it is the difference between three major thirds ($5^3:4^3$ or 125:64) and 2:1. Figure 4.12 shows a subset of the lattice bounded vertically by the great diesis. The tones in the highest and lowest rows of this figure are what conventional theory calls "enharmonic equivalents," pairs of tones that are called by different names depending on the contexts in which they occur,

Figure 4.12: The great or enharmonic diesis

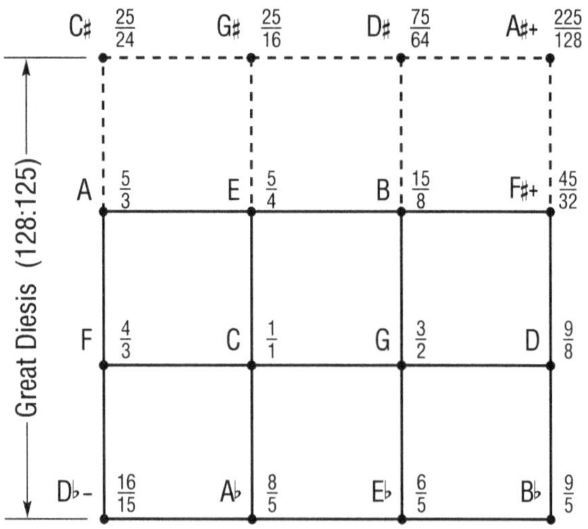

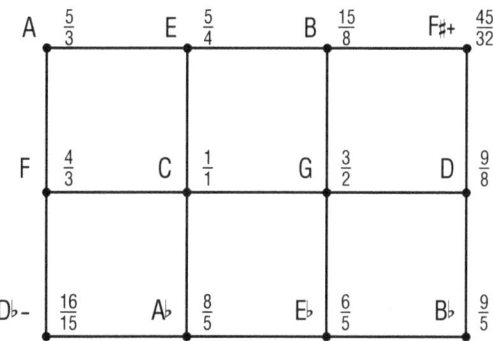

Figure 4.13: The harmonic duodene of C (lattice)

but that, at least on conventional keyboard instruments, are represented by a single tone. Note that the flats in the bottom row are *higher* than the corresponding sharps in the top row by 128:125; the opposite of what one might intuitively expect. Whereas choosing the sharp or flat version of a tone in equal temperament is merely a matter of correct "spelling" that, at least on keyboard instruments, makes no audible difference, in Just Intonation, the choice is extremely significant. Choosing the tone on the wrong side of the diesis, for example, using A♭ 8/5 rather than G♯ 25/16 in a major triad on E 5/4, will produce a truly grating dissonance. In place of the just major and minor thirds, 5:4 and 6:5, this "triad" has the diminished fourth, 32:25, and the augmented second, 75:64. Nevertheless, the great diesis is not generally as troublesome as the syntonic comma, since it occurs between tones that are less likely to occur consecutively in common harmonic progressions. Still, certain of the more radical modulations typical of later common-practice music or contemporary pop music may involve approaching a tone as though it were a flat and leaving it as though it were the "equivalent" sharp. These radical modulations must be treated with considerably more care in Just Intonation.

The Harmonic Duodene

Attempting to create a five-limit tuning which avoids both the great diesis and the syntonic comma results in something closely resembling a twelve-tone chromatic scale. Avoiding the great diesis requires limiting the height of the columns of 5:4s to two links, whereas avoiding the syntonic comma requires limiting adjacent rows of 3:2s to three links. While several tunings can be created which satisfy these conditions, most of them quite bizarre, the most obvious and practical consists of a rectangle defined by three 5:4s by four 3:2s, such as that in Figure 4.13. This type of scale was described by Alexander J. Ellis, English translator and annotator of Helmholtz's *On the Sensations of Tone*, who called it a *harmonic duodene* and considered it the basic unit of modulation for triadic harmony.[6] The scale in Figure 4.13, which Ellis terms "the duodene of C," contains the major and natural minor scales on C (1/1), plus two additional tones, D♭- 16/15 and F♯+ 45/32. It also includes the major scale on A♭ 8/5 and the natural minor on E 5/4. Its chordal resources include six good major triads, on C, D♭-, E♭, F, G, and A♭, and six good minor triads, on C, E, F, G, A, and B. When the duodene is arranged in scale order (Figure 4.14), it is seen to include four different semitones: 25:24, the small just chromatic semitone (70.7 cents); 135:128, the large limma or large chromatic semitone (92.2 cents); 16:15, the just diatonic semitone (111.7 cents); and 27:25, the great limma (133.2 cents). As different in magnitude as these four intervals are, they are all perceptually semitones, and when the entire series is played in scale order, the Western-trained ear accepts it as a chromatic scale.

Nevertheless, the properties of this scale, or of any other possible just scale of twelve tones per octave, are very different from those of the chromatic scale in twelve-tone equal temperament. In equal temperament, a twelve-tone chromatic scale represents the totality of the musical universe. Within the tempered chromatic scale, any melody or harmonic progressions may be transposed to any scale degree and still retain its original intervallic structure. In Just Intonation, a twelve tone scale, however musically useful it may be, is just a small fragment of an infinite tonal space. And any finite just tuning, however large, will contain possible figures that cannot be transposed to other degrees in the system without requiring additional tones. When Ellis termed the duodene "the unit of modulation," he did not

Figure 4.14: The harmonic duodene of C (scale order)

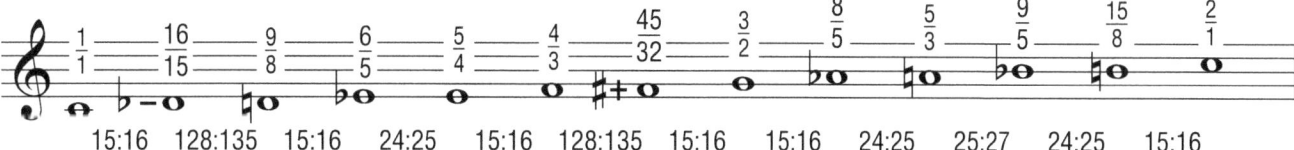

mean that modulation was to occur *within* the duodene, but rather between it and related duodenes centered on other tones. He proposed using a field of 117 tones from the five-limit fabric, arranged in a matrix of nine 3:2s by thirteen 5:4s, which he called "the duodenarium," as being adequate for all of the modulations used in the music of his time (the last quarter of the nineteenth century). Actually, this number of tones is enough to allow for seventy distinct duodenes, a far cry from the traditional twelve major and minor keys, so one suspects that Ellis was being rather liberal in estimating the modulatory requirements even of late romantic music. He does admit, however, that "it is impossible to be certain how far the ambiguities of tempered intonation may mislead the composer to consider as related, chords and scales which are really very far apart."[7] Pretty far, I'm inclined to say. Ellis also fails to address the problems that arise when one tries to map the kind of harmonic progressions that characterize common-practice music onto the five-limit fabric. If he had done so, he might have concluded that *any* plan to transplant the harmonic practices of the late nineteenth century to a just system was futile.

Five Limit Chords

THE MAJOR TRIAD—The five-limit major triad conforms in all respects to our definition of a consonant chord in Just Intonation. Indeed, it is the simplest possible chord having three unique identities, being composed of the identities 1, 3, and 5. In contrast to the Pythagorean major triad, the five-limit major triad is free of disturbing interference beats (assuming a harmonic timbre), and is accompanied by first-order difference tones that reinforce the identity of the series from which the chord derives. In root position, the fifth harmonic of the root (1 identity) coincides with the fourth harmonic of the major third (5 identity), and the sixth harmonic of the major third coincides with the fifth harmonic of the perfect fifth (3 identity). The third harmonic of the root and the second harmonic of the perfect fifth (and their doubles, the sixth and fourth) coincide in both the Pythagorean and the five-limit triads. The three primary difference tones of the five-limit triad further reinforce the 1 identity of the chord. Figure 4.15 shows the first-order difference tones (black note heads) of the just major triad in its three inversions in close position. In all three cases, the difference tones correspond to lower octaves of the 1

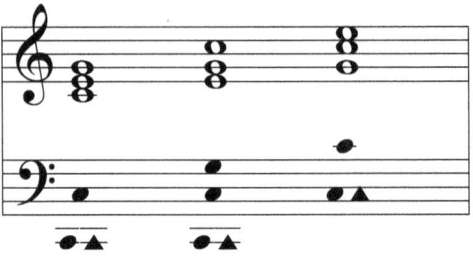

○ = parent   ● = first-order difference tone
▲ = periodicity pitch

Figure 4.15: First-order difference tones and periodicity pitches of the C-major triad

and/or 3 identities. The periodicity pitches of the chords (triangular note heads) also corresponds to the 1 identity of this series. All of these phenomena combine to reinforce the fundamental of the harmonic series from which the chord derives and helps to make it a stable chord with a clear and unambiguous meaning.

THE MINOR TRIAD—The case of the minor triad is more complicated. Indeed, the very nature of the minor triad and of minor harmony in general has been a subject of controversy for at least three hundred years, and this controversy has by no means been resolved as of the time of this writing. The five-limit minor triad is certainly more consonant than the Pythagorean minor, but it is also less consonant than the five-limit major triad, for reasons that will be explained directly. In root position, the tones of the minor triad have, harmonically speaking, the relative frequencies 10:12:15. Factoring out powers of 2, we see that it is composed of the identities 3, 5 and 15, the last being, coincidentally, the product of the first two. Obviously, the minor triad lacks a 1 identity. Of all the possible combinations of three tones that can be made from the first five identities in the five limit (1, 3, 5, 9, 15), only the major and minor triads are unequivocally consonant, regardless of their inversions. This is probably sufficient explanation of the prominent place the minor triad occupies in Western music.

In regard to coincident harmonics, the five-limit minor triad fares as well as the major. In root position, the sixth harmonic of the root (5 identity), the fifth harmonic of the minor third (3 identity) and the fourth harmonic of the perfect fifth (15 identity) are identical. It is the difference tones and periodicity pitch that compromise the consonance of the minor triad. Figure

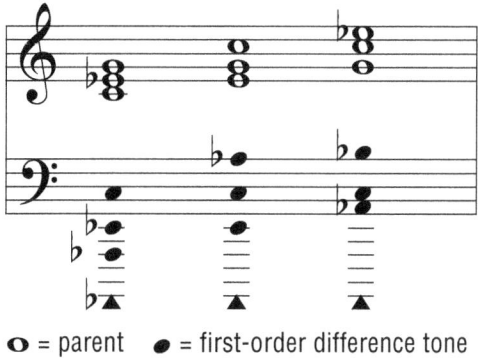

o = parent ● = first-order difference tone
▲ = periodicity pitch

Figure 4.16: First-order difference tones and periodicity pitches of the C-minor triad

4.16 shows the first-order difference tones of the three inversions of the minor triad in close position. In each case, the first order difference tones include one or more tones that are not part of the triad. In particular, all three sets of difference tones include A♭ 8/5, the missing 1 identity. In other words, the C minor triad is composed of the identities 3, 5, and 15 of a harmonic series of which A♭ 8/5 is the fundamental. Thus, the periodicity pitch of the chord also corresponds to A♭.

Many theorists have attempted to explain the minor triad in terms of the subharmonic series. (As explained previously, the subharmonic series is the complement of the harmonic series.) To find the position of any set of just tones in a subharmonic series, convert the ratios to their least common *numerator*. When we perform this operation on any minor triad, we find that it comprises degrees 4, 5, and 6 of a subharmonic series. In other words, the minor triad comprises the subharmonic identities 1, 3, and 5. When the triad is in its root position, the 1 identity is the highest tone in the chord, which conventional music theory calls the fifth of the chord. The fundamental of the subharmonic series to which the minor triad belongs corresponds to the lowest common harmonic shared by all three of the chord's tones. In other words, the generator of what conventional music theory would call a C minor triad is not C, but G. This makes the minor triad the exact complement or mirror image of the major triad. From this fact, many theorists, especially Harry Partch, have concluded that major and minor tonality (in Partchian terms, "otonality" and "utonality") are equal in consonance, equal in musical importance, and equal in their capacity for expansion. The Partchian view, however, ignores the implications of difference tones and periodicity pitches. These phenomena will always reinforce a harmonic interpretation of a chord, as indicated above.

It is really impossible to say, given the current state of psychoacoustic knowledge, which of the explanations of the minor triad is correct, and it is quite conceivable that both explanations contribute to its acceptance by the ear. It is interesting, however, that whichever explanation of the minor triad we accept, in neither case does the tone conventionally identified as the root of the chord correspond to the 1 identity of the series from which the chord derives.

CONDISSONANT CHORDS IN THE FIVE LIMIT

Although the major and minor triads are the only chords in the five limit which are strictly consonant regardless of position or inversion, the five-limit fabric includes a variety of other useful and interesting chords which mix consonant and dissonant elements. Most of these are what conventional theory calls nondominant-seventh or -ninth chords. Although all of these chords contain one or more comparatively dissonant elements, when properly tuned each is a unified and harmonious whole in which consonance predominates, each tone being related to one or more of the others by simple, consonant intervals. The essential unity of each of these chords is confirmed by the fact that they are sensitive to mistuning. Comparatively small alterations in the pitch of a single tone will cause significant damage to the overall unity and stability of any of them. As stated previously, I will follow the example of Ellis and refer to these chords as "condissonant" chords.

CONDISSONANT TRIADS — Although most of the condissonant chords within the five limit involve four or more identities, two are triads of a type not recognized by conventional theory. These two chords have the relative frequencies 8:12:15 (identities 1-3-15) and 8:10:15 (identities 1-5-15) respectively. These are the only chords other than the major and minor triads which comprise three adjacent points on the two axes of the five-limit lattice. This fact alone makes them worthy of special attention. Each includes the two primary intervals 3:2 and 5:4, and their sum, the just diatonic major seventh, 15:8. Though more complex than the major and minor triads, these chords comprise sufficiently low-numbered identities to be comprehensible to the ear. The primary difference tones of these chords serve to reinforce the identity of the harmonic series from which they derive, though in some cases they include the identities 7 or 9, which add additional complexity to the texture.

THE MAJOR-SEVENTH CHORD — When the two types of condissonant triads are combined with a common root, they produce the four-tone chord or tetrad that is known in conventional theory as the major-seventh chord. This chord, which comprises degrees 1, 3, 5, and 7 of the syntonon diatonic, has, in root position, the relative frequencies: 8:10:12:15 (identities 1-5-3-15). It is symmetrical, consisting alternately of two interlocking 3:2s offset by 5:4, or two 5:4s separated by a central 6:5. It can also be viewed as a major triad overlapped by a minor triad beginning on its major third. The major-seventh chord forms a square on the five-limit lattice and constitutes the closest possible interrelationship among four different tones within this limit. This chord has a clearly defined 1 identity which corresponds to its nominal root. Like all four-note chords, the major-seventh chord produces six first-order difference tones, although in some cases two of these overlap, reducing the number of perceived tones to five. In all of its inversions, the first-order difference tones of the major-seventh chord strongly reinforce the root and other lower identities of the series to which the chord belongs. In its root position and third inversion, the first-order difference tones of this chord include the 7 and 9 identities respectively. The presence of these identities may increase the perceived complexity of these two positions slightly, but does not seriously injure their relative consonance.

THE MINOR-SEVENTH CHORD — Another comparatively consonant tetrad found in the five limit is the minor-seventh chord (relative frequencies in root position: 10:12:15:18, identities 5-3-15-9). This chord is also symmetrical, consisting of a pair of interlocking 3:2s offset by 6:5, or of a pair of 6:5s around a central 5:4. It can also be viewed as a minor triad overlapped by a major triad starting on its minor third. The minor-seventh chord can also be found in the syntonon diatonic, comprising degrees 2, 3, 5, and 7. Like the minor triad, the minor-seventh chord lacks a 1 identity, which would be represented by 8 or 16 in the series above. In other words, the missing 1 identity will be found a 5:4 below or an 8:5 above the nominal root. The first-order difference tones of the minor-seventh chord in all positions strongly support the true identity of the series from which the chord derives, the missing 1 identity being strongly represented in all cases. The difference tones add no new identities other than 1. Common-practice harmony usually treats the minor-seventh chord as a major triad with an added sixth. This is particularly true in regard to the first inversion (relative frequencies 12:15:18:20), which places the major triad in root position at the bottom of the chord. Whether the ear really hears this chord as a major triad with an added dissonance or as a series of identities belonging to a missing fundamental is impossible to say with certainty. Undoubtedly the musical context wields considerable influence over how this ambiguous chord will be understood.

THE MAJOR- AND MINOR-NINTH CHORDS —

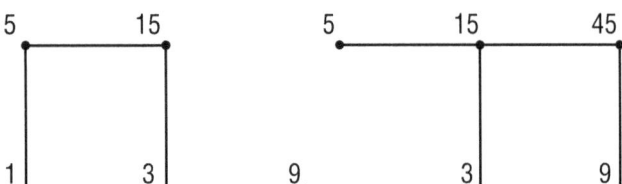

The major-seventh and minor-seventh chords can be overlapped, with the major seventh in the lower position, to create the major-ninth chord (relative frequencies 8:10:12:15:18, identities 1-5-3-15-9). This chord comprises five of the seven tones of the syntonon diatonic, only the fourth and sixth degrees being excluded. It includes three overlapping triads, major-minor-major, and can also be seen as a chain of alternating thirds, major-minor-major-minor. Overlapping the two seventh chords with the minor seventh in the lower position produces the complement of the major-ninth chord, which conventional theory would call a minor-ninth chord. This is a much more complex chord, with the relative frequencies 20:24:30:36:45, representing identities 5-3-15-9-45. This chord also contains three overlapping triads (minor-major-minor) and can be seen as a chain of thirds (minor-major-minor-major).

DEFICIENCIES OF THE FIVE LIMIT

Though the five limit generates many important chords recognized in conventional theory and practice, some others are absent. Among these are the dominant-seventh chord, the diminished triad, the augmented triad, and the diminished-seventh chord. How these chords, which are traditionally explained as various combinations of major and minor thirds, could be absent in an intonational fabric which includes potentially infinite numbers of these intervals requires some explanation. Consider the dominant-seventh chord. This chord is traditionally described as a major triad with an added tone a minor third above the fifth. It is also described as consisting of the fifth, seventh, second, and fourth degrees of the major scale. The first thing to observe is that these two explanations result in two different sevenths when applied to five-limit Just Intonation. In the case of the seventh chord on G, the dominant in the key of C, the tone a 6:5 above the fifth (D $9/8$) is F+ $27/20$. In this case, the interval between the root of the chord and the seventh is 9:5, the acute minor seventh. The fourth degree of the C major scale, on the other hand, is F $4/3$, a Pythagorean minor third (32:27) above D $9/8$ and hence a syntonic comma lower than $27/20$. Using $4/3$ as the seventh of the chord results in a seventh of 16:9. The relative frequencies of the first version are 20:25:30:36, representing identities 5-25-15-9. This chord lacks a 1 identity and is quite dissonant, having the acute diminished fifth, 36:25, in addition to the acute minor seventh. The second version has the relative frequencies 36:45:54:64, representing the identities 9-45-27-1. This chord is, if anything, more dissonant than the first. Further, its 1 identity, the tone that ought to coincide with the root, is in the highest voice in root position, and has the function of an added dissonance. Of course, in conventional theory the dominant-seventh is a dissonant chord which requires resolution, normally to the tonic. From this point of view, either of these chords ought to suffice, but the second ($4/3$) version would probably be preferred as being native to the major scale.

In practice, the dominant-seventh chord receives different treatments in different musical styles. In the earlier part of the common-practice period, the dominant seventh always required preparation and regular (stepwise) resolution. Later, it came to be accepted as an independent sonority that could be used on any scale degree. It is freely used in this way in most styles of contemporary popular music. Under the latter circumstances, it would seem appropriate, in Just Intonation, to use a more consonant tuning for the dominant-seventh chord if one were available. Such a tuning has been known since the eighteenth century. It involves the harmonic seventh, 7:4, taking us beyond the five limit. The harmonic seventh of G $3/2$ is F7+ $21/16$ (3:2 + 7:4), and the resulting chord has the relative frequencies 4:5:6:7 in root position, representing identities 1-5-3-7. This is a far simpler, more consonant chord than either of the alternatives offered by the five limit. Good taste dictates that this version of the dominant-seventh chord ought to be used at least in those situations where resolution is not required. It also performs perfectly well in situations where resolution occurs, despite the fact that it is not in the least dissonant. The diminished triad, being composed of the three higher tones of the dominant-seventh chord, is subject to the same considerations as that chord. Its preferred tuning has the relative frequencies 5:6:7. Thus, while it may not be absolutely accurate to say that no dominant-seventh chords or diminished triads exist in the five limit, the seven-limit versions of these chords offer such superior consonance and clarity that they are to be preferred in almost every case, except perhaps where the seventh is only struck briefly as a passing tone or appoggiatura. The dominant-seventh chord and the diminished triad will be explored in greater detail when we examine the seven limit in the next chapter.

The augmented triad and the diminished-seventh chord are more problematic. In a sense, both of these chords, at least in the way they are used in common-practice harmony, are products of equal temperament. In equal temperament, an octave can be equally divided into three major thirds or four minor thirds. These two divisions define the augmented triad and the diminished-seventh chord, respectively. Since these two chords are composed, in equal temperament, of identical intervals, their intervallic structures remain the same when inverted and their true roots cannot be identified except from the contexts in which they appear. Further, there are only four unique augmented triads and three unique diminished-seventh chords in twelve-tone equal temperament, though each may have a variety of "enharmonic spellings." These properties make these two chords useful as pivots for modulation to relatively remote tonal centers.

One can make a variety of chords in Just Intonation that the ear will accept as augmented triads or diminished-seventh chords, but they will not have the same properties as the tempered versions of those chords, since those properties are consequences of equal temperament. In Just Intonation, every chord can be analyzed as a harmonic series segment, and will therefore imply a fundamental, though the chord may be too complex for that fundamental to be easily identified by the ear. No chord in Just Intonation will retain the same intervallic structure when inverted, because no chord in Just Intonation, by definition, can divide an octave into any number of equal intervals. Consider, for example, the augmented triad. In conventional theory, an augmented triad is composed of two consecutive major thirds. Therefore, we ought, in Just Intonation, to build such a chord from two 5:4s. Starting on $1/1$, this would give us the three tones C $1/1$, E $5/4$, and G♯ $25/16$. This is a rather dissonant chord that doesn't sound much different from a tempered augmented triad. Structurally, however, there are significant differences. First, this chord has the relative frequencies 16:20:25, representing the identities 1-5-25, so there's absolutely no ambiguity as to which tone is the fundamental. Second, the intervallic structure is different for each of the three inversions. In root position, the intervals between the tones are both 5:4s and the outer interval is 25:16. In the first inversion (20:25:32) the intervals between tones are a 5:4 below and a 32:25 above, and the outer interval is 8:5. In the second inversion (25:32:40) the inner intervals are a 32:25 below and a 5:4 above and the outer interval is again an 8:5. Most important, this chord cannot possibly function as an augmented triad in equal temperament does. In equal temperament, the chord C-E-G♯ cannot be distinguished from C-E-A♭ except by means of context. Thus a tempered augmented triad on C could as easily move to E major, by moving the root down by a semitone, or to A♭ major, by moving the third down a semitone. This is, of course, not possible in Just Intonation, since G♯ and A♭ are two distinct tones which, at least in this particular context, differ by the great diesis, 128:125. The triad C-E-G♯ in Just Intonation can readily move to B-E-G♯ in the manner described above, but in order to move to C-E♭-A♭, the G♯ $25/16$ must be raised by 128:125 (approximately 41 cents) to A♭ $8/5$ while the E $5/4$ descends by 25:24 to E♭ $6/5$. This kind of microtonal voice leading is certainly possible in Just Intonation, and may be desirable in some situations, but it has quite a different effect than the practice of using a single tempered tone under two different names.

The diminished-seventh chord in equal temperament consists of three successive minor thirds, so we might attempt to build such a chord in Just Intonation out of three 6:5s. Starting on C $1/1$, this would yield the tones C $1/1$, E♭ $6/5$, G♭ $36/25$, and B♭♭ $216/125$. These four tones have the relative frequencies 125:150:180:216 and correspond to the identities 125-75-45-27 of a missing fundamental, $128/125$. I think we can be confident that no listener can comprehend a series of high number identities such as these. The interval between B♭♭ $216/125$ and C $2/1$ is not 6:5 but rather 125:108, approximately 253.1 cents, so this chord, like our augmented triad above, will have a different intervallic structure for each of its inversions.

Conventional theory explains the diminished-seventh chord as a dominant-minor-ninth chord with the root missing. From this point of view, a diminished-seventh chord on C $1/1$ would be part of a dominant-minor-ninth on A♭ $8/5$. Although C $1/1$ and E♭ $6/5$ are proper constituents of such a chord, the remaining tones are not. As stated above, the preferred seventh for chords of dominant function is the harmonic seventh, 7:4. The harmonic seventh of $8/5$ is G♭7, $7/5$. What about the minor ninth? This is an interval that we haven't dealt with previously. In conventional theory, a minor ninth is simply the sum of a minor second and an octave. In Just Intonation, there are many kinds of minor seconds. I will dispense with the process of testing all of the possible minor seconds/ninths relative to $8/5$ in the five limit to see which might yields the most satisfactory diminished-seventh chord, and tell you that the best choice for a minor ninth, that is, the tone that yields the smallest numbers for the relative frequencies and the corresponding identities, is 17:8, an octave expansion of the primary interval for the prime 17. Using this interval in combination with the harmonic seventh yields a diminished-seventh chord with the relative frequencies 10:12:14:17 (identities 5-3-7-17), a far more comprehensible and harmonious chord than that created from a chain of 6:5s, as well as one in which the root that classical theory expects corresponds to the fundamental of the series. A diminished-seventh chord of this type on C $1/1$ would have the tones C $1/1$, E♭ $6/5$, G♭ $7/5$ and A17 $17/10$. The addition of an A♭ $8/5$ below would make a complete dominant-minor-ninth chord. This chord, while it is an interesting sonority and may have a role to play in some styles of music in Just Intonation, has none of the properties of the tempered diminished-seventh chord. Its root is clear and its intervallic structure is different for each of its inversions. It is therefore no more suitable as a pivot for obscure modulations than is the augmented triad discussed above.

THE LADDER OF PRIMES, PART TWO: SEVEN AND BEYOND

SEVEN-LIMIT INTERVALS

NEW CONSONANCES

The primary interval for 7 is 7:4, known as the harmonic seventh or septimal minor seventh. This interval represents a greater departure from familiar musical materials than the intervals of the five limit. At 968.8 cents, it is approximately 31 cents narrower than the tempered minor seventh, more than twice the deviation of the just thirds and sixths from their tempered "equivalents." More important, 7:4 is a powerful consonance, whereas tempered, three-limit, and five-limit minor sevenths are all quite dissonant. Thus the harmonic use of 7:4 demands a departure from common-practice. As stated previously, 7:4 is a necessary constituent of consonant dominant-seventh chords and diminished triads.

The complement of 7:4 is 8:7, the supermajor second (231.2 cents). Although this interval is too narrow to be a consonance because it falls within the critical band throughout the musically useful frequency range, it is nevertheless an important interval for chord and scale construction.

Although consonant dominant-seventh chords and diminished triads may be the most obvious reasons for admitting the prime number 7 to our tonal universe, the resources provided by 7 extend far beyond these familiar chords. When we add 7:4 to the two-dimensional five-limit fabric, it is transformed into a three-dimensional lattice containing a number of other unique intervals based on 7. A portion of this infinite lattice is illustrated in Figure 5.1a The horizontal and vertical axes retain the meanings they had in the five-limit lattice we examined previously. Figure 5.1b shows another view of the lattice, "exploded" on the 5 axis to make four links on the 7 axis visible without too much clutter. Each link on the new diagonal (front-to-back) axis represents 7:4 and/or its complement 8:7. Thus, three integers are required to describe any interval in the seven limit in terms of its position on the lattice. For example, the harmonic seventh (7:4) would be represented as (0, 0, 1), meaning that this interval requires no steps on the horizontal or vertical axes and one positive step (toward the upper left) on the diagonal axis. Its complement, 8:7, the supermajor second, would be represented as (0, 0, –1). Figure 5.1b shows an area bounded by six perfect fifths (3:2s), four major thirds (5:4s), and four harmonic sevenths (7:4s).

The most important new intervals in the seven-limit lattice, after 7:4, are 7:5 (582.5 cents), the most consonant of the many possible just tritones, and 7:6 (266.9 cents), a small minor third, generally called a subminor third or septimal minor third. 7:4, 7:5, and 7:6 can be identified with the flatted seventh, fifth, and third beloved of blues and jazz musicians. All three are quite consonant, but possess a distinctive quality not found in five-limit intervals. The octave extensions of 7:4 and 7:6, 7:2 and 7:3, are also strong consonances. The octave extension of 7:5, 14:5, is weakly consonant at best. The complements of 7:6 and 7:5, 12:7 and 10:7, are also only marginally consonant.

In addition to providing a number of new consonances, the seven limit introduces numerous smaller intervals (whole tones, semitones, and microtones) that are useful for melody and/or harmonic voice leading. (Each of these intervals can be found, along with its cents value and lattice position, in Table 5.1, below. It will be helpful to trace each of the intervals presented here on the lattice in Figures 5.1a and 5.1b, in order to better understand how each is the sum of a small number of primary intervals.)

Table 5.1. Seven-limit tones, semitones, and microtones

Ratio	Cents	Lattice Position
8:7	231.2	(0, 0, –1)
28:25	196.2	(0, –2, 1)
35:32	155.1	(0, 1, 1)
15:14	119.4	(1, 1, –1)
21:20	84.5	(1, –1, 1)
28:27	63.0	(–3, 0, 1)
36:35	48.8	(2, –1, –1)
49:48	35.7	(–1, 0, 2)
50:49	35.0	(0, 2, –2)
64:63	27.3	(–2, 0, –1)

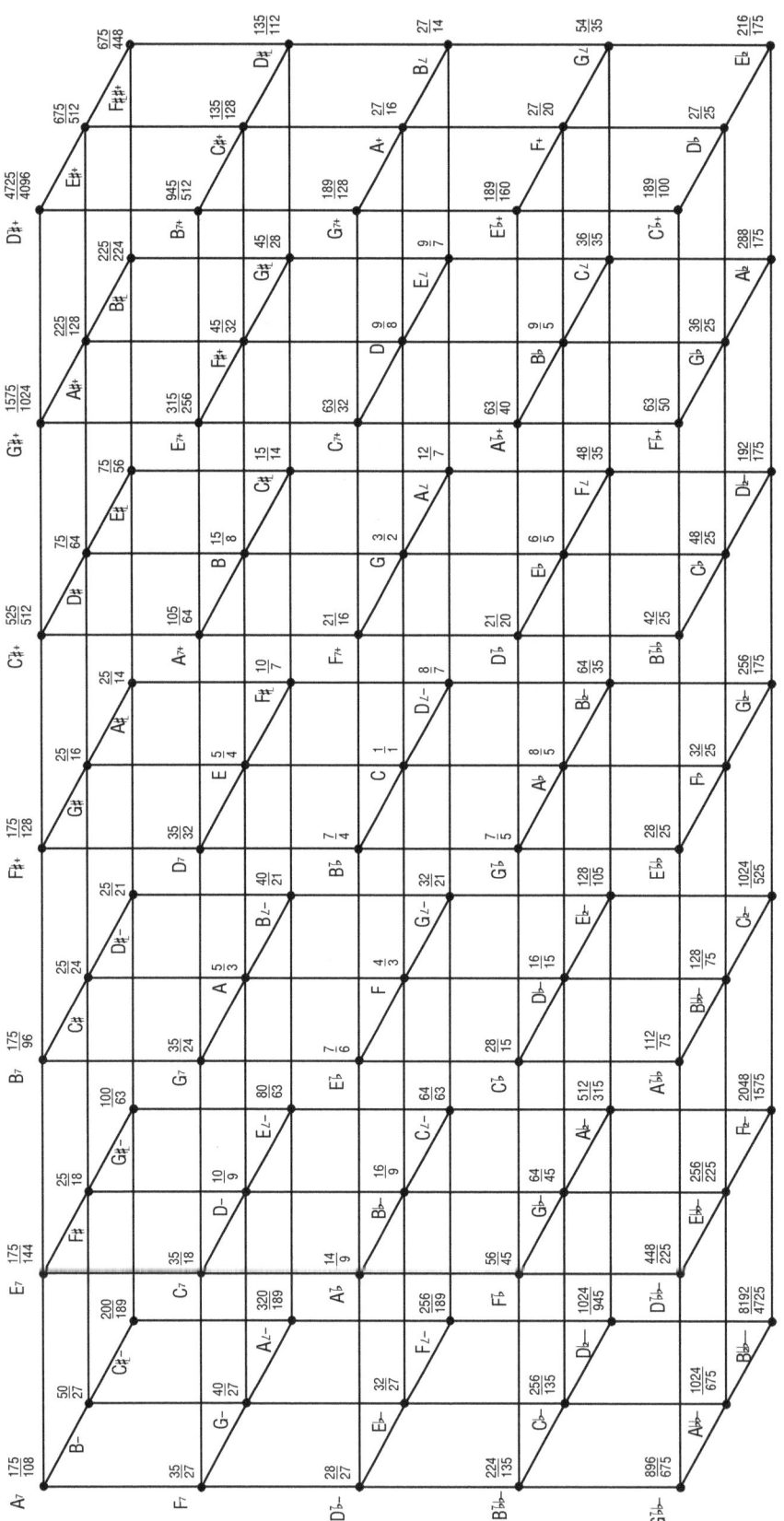

Figure 5.1a: Seven-limit lattice

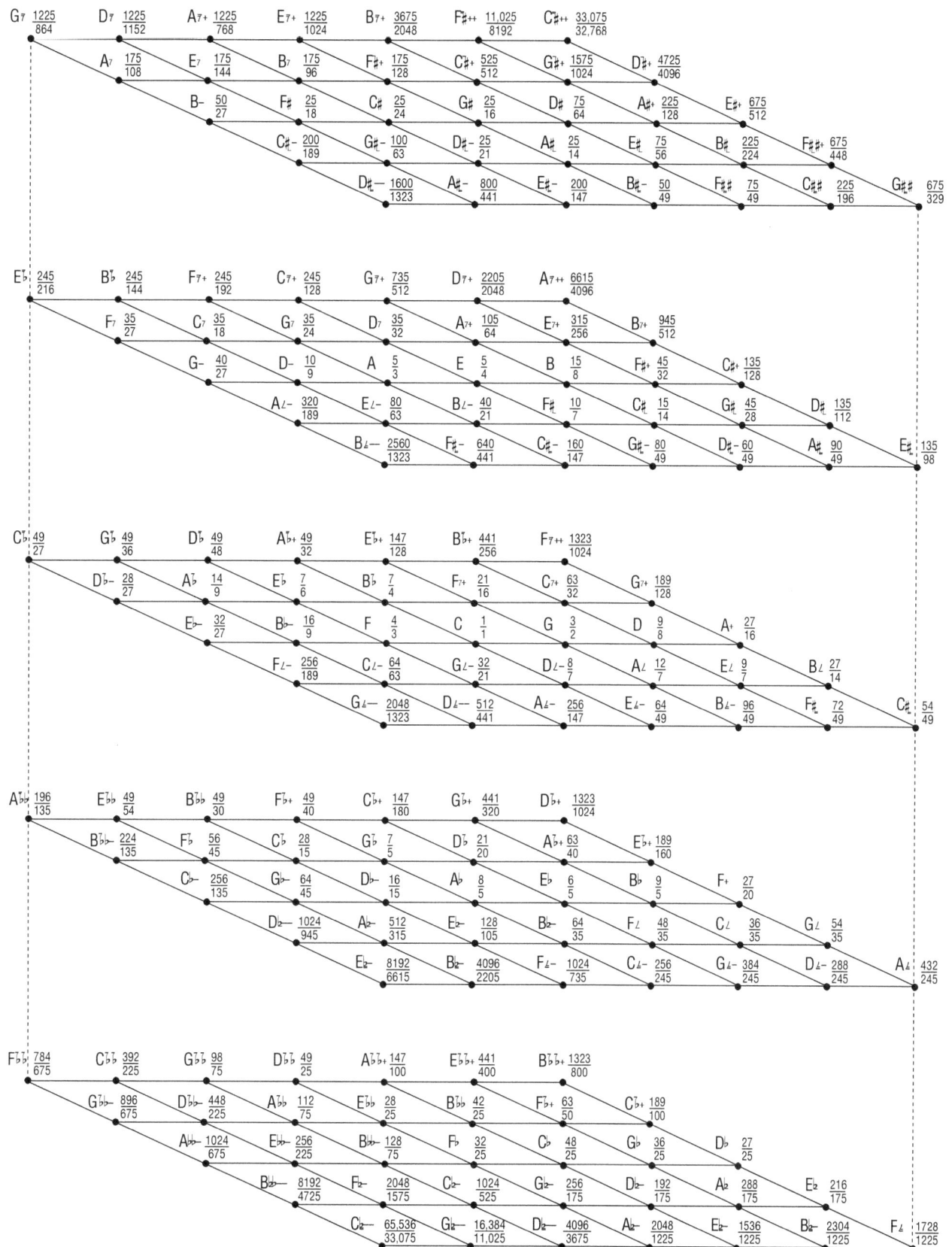

Figure 5.1b: Seven-limit lattice "exploded" on the five axis

WHOLE TONES

We have already mentioned 8:7, the complement of 7:4, which is variously known as the supermajor second, septimal wholetone, or maximum wholetone. This interval is an important component of many seven-limit tetrachordal scales. A more obscure wholetone interval is 28:25, which Ralph David Hill has christened the "intermediate septimal whole tone."[1] At 196.2 cents, this interval closely approximates the equally tempered major second. So far as I have discovered, this interval was not used in any of the ancient tetrachordal scales. Not being superparticular, it probably had two strikes against it in the minds of the ancient Greek harmonists. The intermediate septimal whole tone appears occasionally as a voice-leading interval in seven-limit harmonic music. In order of decreasing interval size, we next encounter 35:32, which Hill calls the small septimal whole tone. At approximately 155.1 cents, this interval actually ought to be called a neutral second. It stands in a perceptual no-man's-land between the whole tones and the semitones, and is quite foreign sounding to Western-trained ears. This interval is also absent from the ancient tetrachordal scales, but is a useful voice leading interval in seven-limit harmonic music.

SEMITONES

In the semitone category are, in order of diminishing size, 15:14, 21:20, and 28:27. These three intervals are used in various diatonic and chromatic scales reported by the ancient Greek and Islamic theorists. They are also common voice-leading intervals in seven-limit harmonic music. Although these three intervals differ considerably in magnitude, with 15:14 being almost twice the size of 28:27, all three ought, in my opinion, to be considered semitones. All are capable of functioning as such in the various ancient diatonic and chromatic scales illustrated in Figure 5.2. You may, of course, label 28:27 as a "third tone" if you wish.

MICROTONES

The seven limit provides at least four significant microtones: 36:35, the septimal quarter tone or diesis; 49:48 and 50:49, septimal sixth tones; and 64:63, the septimal comma. Each of these microtones, has, of course, a complement that can be called an augmented seventh or diminished octave. These microtones (with the exception of 50:49) also occur in a variety of ancient tetrachordal scales.[2]

Both the septimal semitones and the septimal microtones occur as voice-leading intervals when chords having 7 identities progress by simple intervals, or when triads progress by intervals involving 7. Observe that each of these microtones involves four or fewer steps on the lattice. Thus, they are readily comprehensible as products of a small number of simple, consonant intervals. All of these intervals are, perhaps not coincidentally, superparticular. There are, of course, many other small intervals in the seven limit, as there are, indeed, within any prime limit, but these intervals are probably too obscure to be of immediate interest.

FALSE CONSONANCES

There are a few other intervals within the seven limit that are worthy of special attention. Perhaps the most significant of these are the septimal subfourth, 21:16 (470.8 cents), and its complement 32:21 (729.2 cents). These intervals are equivalent to a perfect fourth (4:3) diminished by a septimal comma (64:63), or a perfect fifth (3:2) augmented by that same interval. Although these intervals are quite simple in terms of location on the lattice, being (1, 0, 1) and (–1, 0, –1) respectively, they are certainly not consonant. In my opinion, they are perfect examples of the phenomenon known as "false consonance." The theory of false consonance, first propounded by Miles Maxwell in 1973,[3] states that intervals that are too close in size to certain powerful consonances cannot be understood or appreciated for their own sake, but will be perceived as distortions of their more consonant neighbors. These intervals are distinct from ordinary dissonances, which, while not consonant, are not mistaken for anything else, and therefore do not cause such confusion. Maxwell proposes a set of limits for how close various consonances can be approached without creating false consonances. For the perfect fourth and fifth, the forbidden zone is 28:27 (63 cents). 21:16 and 32:21 fall well inside this limit, being only a septimal comma removed from the perfect fourth and perfect fifth, respectively. Without necessarily embracing all of Maxwell's conclusions, I must agree that 21:16 is clearly a false fourth, and its complement 32:21 is a false fifth. I generally find these intervals unacceptable as unsupported harmonic intervals or in unaccompanied melody. Harmonically, these intervals may be able to function satisfactorily in the context of certain condissonant chords where the 21 identity is supported by the identities that are its factors, 3 and 7, in addition to 1. Chords of this type have not been sufficiently explored to allow a conclusion to be drawn. One area where I do find 21:16 or 32:21 acceptable is as an interval for root movement of chords. It is possible to move dominant-seventh or dominant-ninth chords by this interval in such a manner that all of the voices progress by simple, smooth intervals.

Another interval that partakes, to a degree, of the properties of false consonance is 9:7, the supermajor third (435.1 cents). When sounded alone as a harmonic interval, 9:7 may be perceived as a false major third (5:4); it doesn't seem to present any problems when used melodically. It also performs acceptably in chords where other identities help to clarify its role, for example, the dominant-ninth chord (4:5:6:7:9) the half-diminished-seventh chord (5:6:7:9), and the subminor triad (6:7:9). In all three of these chords, the 9 identity is connected to the 3 identity (6) by a perfect fifth (3:2), and the 7 identity is related to the 3 identity by 7:6. Thus, 9:7 is "explained" by these simpler intervals, and is therefore in no danger of being mistaken for a 5:4. Once the ear has been introduced to 9:7 by the use of these chords on particular roots, it may be possible for 9:7 to be used without harmonic support without it being perceived as a false consonance.

Obviously, navigating within the three-dimensional fabric of the seven limit presents even greater complexities than we encountered in the five limit. If five-limit triadic harmony refuses to fit neatly into the world of fixed diatonic or chromatic scales, harmonic music based on the dominant-seventh chord and its subsets and extensions is even less amenable to such constraints. Of course, there are numerous valid compositional approaches to the seven limit. One can explore the various historical pentatonic and heptatonic scales found in the seven-limit fabric or invent one's own scales based on similar principles. It is also possible to add a limited selection of seven-limit intervals for coloristic purposes in a musical texture in which intervals based on 3 and 5 predominate. Such tones can be added for melodic purposes, as inflections or "blue notes," or they can be part of the occasional dominant-seventh or dominant-ninth chord, or diminished triad. When seven-limit intervals are used in this way, the musical fabric remains essentially two dimensional, with the seven-limit tones being appendages or extensions of what is a fundamentally five-limit fabric. Such an approach requires the addition of a relatively small number of additional tones to five-limit fixed scale, assuming one wants to play in only a few closely related keys.

The most challenging approach to composing in the seven limit, and also the one that is likely to yield the most exciting results, is to compose polyphonic or harmonic music in which melodies, chord progressions, and even tonal centers move in all three dimensions of the seven-limit fabric, free from the restrictions of any fixed tuning system. Placing seven-limit intervals on a structurally equal footing with the more familiar intervals of the five limit almost inevitably leads to microtonality, because the various microtonal intervals described above inevitably arise in voice-leading situations when triads and dominant-seventh and -ninth chords progress by intervals such as 7:4, 7:5, 7:6, 9:7, and 21:16.

Two Dimensional Planes in the Seven-Limit Fabric

The seven-limit lattice, being a solid, can be viewed as being composed of three types of two-dimensional planes, at 90 degree angles to one another. Each type of plane is generated by two prime numbers. We have already examined one such plane, that generated by the primes 3 and 5, which is simply the five-limit fabric. The seven-limit lattice contains several duplicates (potentially an infinite number) of this plane, separated from one another by 7:4 or 8:7. The other two planes are, of course, generated by the prime pairs (3, 7) and (5, 7). Scales based on products of 3 and 7 are more comprehensible and more musically useful than those based on 5 and 7. This is because 3 generates the perfect fifth (3:2), the perfect fourth (4:3), and the major whole tone (9:8). Thus, scales including 3 as a factor can use the familiar tetrachordal framework common to Western diatonic scales and include the 3 identity, which plays a powerful role in defining tonality. The principal consonances of the (3, 7) plane, in addition to the perfect fifth and perfect fourth, are 7:4 and 7:6. The most consonant chords in this plane are 4:6:7 and 6:7:9. The (3, 7) plane is replicated at intervals of 5:4 or 8:5 in the seven limit lattice, as seen in Figure 5.1b.

The (5, 7) plane lacks perfect fourths and fifths, major whole tones, and minor (10:9) whole tones. The only simple whole tone in the plane is 8:7. It doesn't include any of the more common types of semitones, such as 16:15, 15:14, 21:20, 25:24, or 28:27, all of which have 3 as a factor. Thus, it is very difficult to construct any familiar scale types in this plane. The only consonant intervals in the (5, 7) plane are 5:4 and 8:5, 7:5 and 7:4, and (marginally) 10:7. The most consonant chord in the plane is a "triad" with the relative frequencies 4:5:7, essentially a dominant-seventh chord with the perfect fifth missing. It seems doubtful, due to this lack of familiar resources, that the (5, 7) plane could form the basis of extended musical compositions. However, it is worth exploring as a source of contrasts to the more familiar patterns available in the (3, 5) and (3, 7) planes.

Seven Limit Chords

The Dominant-Seventh Chord

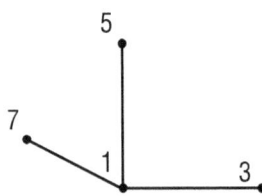

The most important chord in the seven limit is unquestionably the dominant-seventh chord. To make a dominant-seventh chord, we add a harmonic seventh (7:4) above the root to a major triad. The resulting chord has the relative frequencies 4:5:6:7 in root position, representing the identities 1-5-3-7. This is the most consonant possible chord consisting of four unique identities. It has an unambiguous root corresponding to the fundamental of the series from which it derives (the tone designated by 4). The difference tones of the just dominant-seventh chord strongly reinforce the 1 and 3 identities of the series from which the chord derives, adding to its stability and clarity. In no case do they contribute any additional identities not already present in the chord.

In addition to the harmonic seventh, the dominant-seventh chord contains two other consonant intervals involving 7: 7:5 and 7:6. Although the just dominant-seventh chord is unequivocally consonant, it is nevertheless readily identified as a dominant-seventh chord, and provides the needed drive for resolution in V⁷–I cadences. This resolution can be explained in terms of movement from higher identities to lower identities, 1-3-5-7 of the dominant being equivalent to 3-9-15-21 of the tonic.

The Dominant-Ninth chord

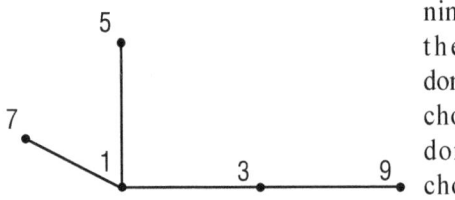

If we add a major ninth (9:4) above the root to a dominant-seventh chord, we get a dominant-ninth chord, with the relative frequencies 4:5:6:7:9 in root position (identities 1-5-3-7-9). Although 9 is an odd number identity, it is, of course, not prime, being the square of 3. The 9 identity is a constituent of some of the condissonant chords in the five limit, such as the minor-seventh chord and major- and minor-ninth chords. The major ninth, taken alone, is a weak consonance or a mild dissonance. The first coincident harmonics resulting from this interval are the ninth of the root and the fourth of the ninth. In most timbres, the ninth harmonic is likely to be too weak to create a very strong impression. Depending on the register in which the major ninth is sounded, beating may occur between some of the lower harmonics of a pair of tones in this relation, adding roughness to the interval. When added to the dominant-seventh chord, the major ninth spawns another relatively dissonant interval, the acute minor seventh, 9:5. Nevertheless, the overall impression created by the just dominant-ninth chord, at least in root position, is one of stability. As with the dominant-seventh chord, the difference tones of the dominant-ninth strongly reinforce the lower identities of the series from which the chord derives, especially the 1 and 3 identities.

Several of the inversions of the dominant-ninth chord in close position include clusters of two or more successive seconds. The second and third inversions, in particular, contain the cluster 7:8:9:10. While a tight cluster like this is strongly dissonant, it also has an orderly, balanced character, as a result of being a succession of degrees of a harmonic series. It is quite different in effect from an analogous cluster of tempered major seconds. The dominant-ninth chord contains an additional interval involving 7, 9:7, the supermajor third. As mentioned previously, 9:7, when heard alone, is a rather marginal consonance, with a tendency to be mistaken for a badly tuned 5:4, but in the context of chords such as the dominant-ninth and its subsets, which include several lower identities, it is quite stable and unambiguous in meaning.

Subsets of the Dominant-Seventh and -Ninth Chords

Most of the other meaningful chords in the seven limit are subsets of the dominant-seventh chord or the dominant-ninth chord. These include chords that are familiar from conventional theory, such as the diminished triad (5:6:7 — identities 5-3-7) and the half-diminished seventh (m7♭5) chord (5:6:7:9 — identities 5-3-7-9), in addition to some combinations that conventional theory does not recognize. One of the most useful nonstandard chords in the seven limit is the thus-far unnamed combination with the relative frequencies

Diminished Triad

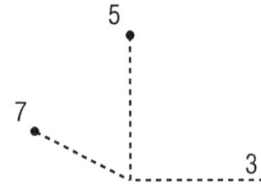

HALF-DIMINISHED SEVENTH CHORD

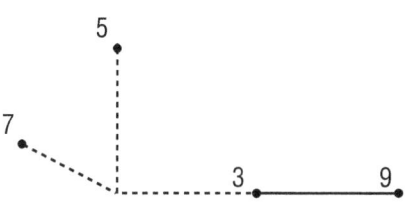

4:6:7 (identities 1-3-7). Conventional theory would call this an incomplete dominant-seventh chord, if it named it at all, but the equivalent combination of root, fifth, and seventh is generally avoided in common-practice harmony; combinations having the tritone are preferred where a dominant-seventh function is required in a three-voice texture. In seven-limit Just

"4-6-7" CHORD

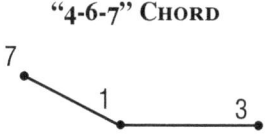

Intonation, this is an extremely consonant chord, perhaps second only to the major triad. Because it lacks the 5 identity and the resulting tritone, it possesses very little dominant-seventh feeling. Its first inversion, 6:7:8, though somewhat more tense due to the narrowness of the supermajor second, 8:7, is still quite a good chord. It is notable in that it constitutes the simplest possible division of the perfect fourth (6:8 = 3:4) by its arithmetic mean, 7:6. The second inversion of this chord, 7:8:12, which puts 7 in the bass voice, isn't nearly as smooth as the other two positions, having both the smaller interval and the highest identity in the lowest position. It will generally be found that chords involving higher identities will be most stable in root position and least stable in voicings that put the highest identity in the bass. This is consistent with common-practice theory. The other three-tone subset of the dominant-seventh, 4:5:7, is much more obviously an incomplete dominant-seventh chord, due to the presence of the tritone 7:5. Aside from being consonant, this combination does not have any special properties in Just Intonation, so far as I have been able to discover.

THE ADDED-SECOND CHORD — Yet another possible subset of the dominant-ninth chord is that with relative frequencies 8:9:10:12 (identities 1-9-5-3). Conventional theory would call this an added-second chord, the term ninth chord normally being reserved for chords which also include the seventh. In Just Intonation, the added second (9 identity) can be seen as a logical extension of the tonality of the chord rather than as an arbitrary added dissonance.

THE SUBMINOR TRIAD — Another powerful and effective combination is 6:7:9 (identities 3-7-9), which I call a subminor or septal minor triad. This chord is quite distinct from the five-limit minor triad (10:12:15) and is, in the opinions of some listeners, more consonant. It is also quite different in the implications suggested by its periodicity pitch. As we learned earlier, the five-limit minor triad has an implied fundamental a 5:4 below the root (in the case of C $^1/_1$ minor, A♭ $^8/_5$). The septal minor triad, in contrast, implies a fundamental a 3:2 below the root, that is, the root of the dominant-ninth chord of which the septal minor is a subset (in the case of C $^1/_1$ subminor, F $^4/_3$). On the whole, this is an extremely useful chord in almost any musical texture in which 7 is featured prominently. In systems based on the primes 3 and 7 without 5, it is the most consonant chord after 4:6:7. In systems based on 3, 5, and 7, it provides a powerful contrast to the five-limit minor triad, almost as powerful as the contrast between minor and major. Conventional theory, of course, doesn't recognize any such entity as a subminor triad. In equal temperament, the upper three tones of a dominant-ninth chord constitute a minor triad like any other. We cannot, therefore, expect common-practice harmony to provide any models of how this chord should behave. Discovering its special properties is one of the necessary steps in creating an appropriate harmonic language for seven-limit Just Intonation.

THE "5:7:9" CHORD — The combination with the relative frequencies 5:7:9 incorporates those elements in the dominant-ninth chord

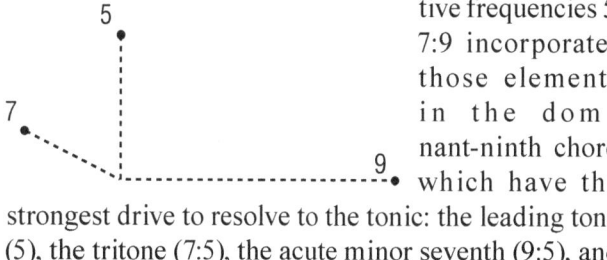

which have the strongest drive to resolve to the tonic: the leading tone (5), the tritone (7:5), the acute minor seventh (9:5), and the supermajor third (9:7). This is an extremely tense sounding chord, even in root position.

SEVEN-LIMIT SUBHARMONIC CHORDS

The equivalent of a dominant-ninth chord can also be constructed from the subharmonic series. Taking C $^1/_1$ as the fundamental of the series, this chord would be composed, in descending order, of the tones C $^1/_1$, A♭ $^8/_5$, F $^4/_3$, D↓ $^8/_7$, and B♭- $^{16}/_9$. These tones have the relative frequencies $^1/_4$:$^1/_5$:$^1/_6$:$^1/_7$:$^1/_9$, and represent the subharmonic identities 1-5-3-7-9. (In Partch's terminology, this would be called a "utonality pentad.") This chord has, of course, subsets equivalent to all of those described above for the harmonic dominant-ninth chord. To the extent that consonance and chordal meaning are influenced by difference tones and periodicity pitch, which are always the products of a harmonic interpretation of a concatenation of tones, the subharmonic pentad and its subsets must be considered inferior to their harmonic equivalents. Where relative consonance is concerned, experience bears this out. The subharmonic pentad on $1/1$, when interpreted as a harmonic series segment, has the relative frequencies 315:252:210:180:140 (identities 315-63-105-45-35) from a harmonic series based on $512/315$ (840.95 cents, a neutral sixth relative to C $1/1$, and a very close approximation to $13/8$, the harmonic 13 identity of $1/1$). Of the ten first-order difference tones that this chord can generate, three correspond to chord tones, whereas the remainder include a broad selection of high and low numbered identities of the harmonic series on $512/315$. Based on this information, it is hard to consider the subharmonic pentad as anything other than a sonic muddle. At least where sustained tones are concerned, the ear tends to support this conclusion.

Of course, none of the subsets of the subharmonic dominant-ninth chord are quite as obscure as their parent. Nevertheless they are all more complex and equivocal than the equivalent harmonic-series segments. Several examples are shown in Table 5.2. The two simplest chords in this table, the so-called "supermajor triad" (named by analogy to the subminor triad, the harmonic 6:7:9 chord) and the subharmonic 4:6:7 chord may be simple and comprehensible enough to function at least as voice-leading chords between more consonant harmonic-series-based chords in the seven limit. It is doubtful, however, whether either could serve as a consonant chord at a point of rest. Both are too obscure in terms of their periodicity pitches for this purpose. The supermajor triad is most likely to be perceived as a false or mistuned major triad, because 9:7 is too close to the more powerful consonance 5:4, and because the chord lacks the lower identities necessary to prevent such confusion.

Table 5.2: Seven-limit subharmonic chords

Subharmonic Tetrad					
Tone	$2/1$	$8/5$	$4/3$	$8/7$	Fundamental
Harmonic Frequency	105	84	70	60	
Harmonic Identity	105	21	35	15	$128/105$
Subharmonic Frequency	4	5	6	7	
Subharmonic Identity	1	5	3	7	$2/1$
Subharmonic Diminished Triad					
Tone	$8/5$	$4/3$	$8/7$	—	Fundamental
Harmonic Frequency	42	35	30	—	
Harmonic Identity	21	35	15	—	$128/105$
Subharmonic Frequency	5	6	7	—	
Subharmonic Identity	1	3	7	—	$2/1$
Supermajor Triad					
Tone	$4/3$	$8/7$	$16/9$	—	Fundamental
Harmonic Frequency	21	18	14	—	
Harmonic Identity	21	9	7	—	$64/63$
Subharmonic Frequency	6	7	9	—	
Subharmonic Identity	3	7	9	—	$2/1$
Subharmonic 4:6:7 Chord					
Tone	$2/1$	$4/3$	$8/7$	—	Fundamental
Harmonic Frequency	21	14	12	—	
Harmonic Identity	21	7	3	—	$32/21$
Subharmonic Frequency	4	6	7	—	
Subharmonic Identity	1	3	7	—	$2/1$

CONDISSONANT CHORDS IN THE SEVEN LIMIT

THE SUBMINOR-SEVENTH CHORD— Other chords in the seven limit that are not subsets of the dominant-seventh chord or dominant-ninth chord can be created by adding higher identities to some of the simpler chords that we have previously examined. For example, the subminor triad can be expanded to a subminor-seventh chord (relative frequencies in root position 12:14:18:21; identities 3-7-9-21) by the addition of a perfect fifth above the 7 identity ($7 \times 3 = 21$). This chord, like the five-limit minor seventh chord, is symmetrical, at least in root position. It can be viewed as two overlapping perfect fifths offset by 7:6 or as two 7:6s surrounding a central 9:7. Observe that this chord has, as its highest three degrees, a supermajor triad. The presence of the 3 identity in the root helps to make the function of the 9 identity clear and thereby diminishes the likelihood of 9:7 being mistaken for a mistuned 5:4 in this situation.

The Supermajor-Seventh Chord—

Adding a 3:2 above the supermajor third of the supermajor triad yields what may be called a supermajor-seventh chord (relative frequencies 14:18:21:27, identities 7-9-21-27). This is also a symmetrical chord, consisting of two perfect fifths offset by 9:7, or two 9:7s surrounding a central 7:6. The additional tone seems to improve this chord's consonance somewhat, but cannot wholly overcome the roughness of the unsupported 9:7. A subminor seventh chord and a supermajor seventh chord can be combined to create what might be called subminor-ninth chord. This chord has the relative frequencies 12:14:18:21:27 in root position, representing the identities 3-7-9-21-27, and can be understood as two subminor triads joined conjunctly.

This whole structure could be extended downward by adding the missing identities 1 and 5 to create a chord with the relative frequencies 8:10:12:14:18:21:27. Conventional theory would call this some kind of thirteenth chord, but we will not use this term in order to avoid confusion with chords involving the prime identity 13. The same procedure can be applied to the dominant-seventh and dominant-ninth chords, even though these chords already include a 1 identity. As mentioned at the beginning of this section, the dominant-seventh and dominant-ninth chords, in addition to being understood as identities 1-5-3-7-(9) of their normal roots, can also be understood as identities 3-15-12-21-(27) of a root a 3:2 lower. This perceptual ambiguity is an important factor in the phenomenon of resolution, and hence is a vital force in the development of tonal music. If we multiply the relative frequencies of the dominant-seventh/-ninth chord by 3, we get the series 12:15:18:21:(27). To this can be added the missing identities 1 and 5, to create a chord with the relative frequencies 8:10:12:15:18:21:(27) (identities 1-5-3-15-9-21-27). This chord differs by only one tone (15) from that created above by adding the missing lower identities to the subminor seventh chord. To be sure, these chords are rather thick in texture and are perhaps near the borderline where comprehensibility is concerned. They can, however, be "filtered" to produce some new subsets that don't belong to the dominant-seventh/-ninth or subminor-seventh/-ninth chords.

It may be possible to build other useful condissonant chords which combine higher identities from the five and seven limits. For example, chords could be built which include both the 7 and 15 identities, that is, both the harmonic (minor) seventh and the diatonic major seventh, but this possibility has, to the best of my knowledge, been little explored.

Fixed Scales in the Seven Limit

The number 7 was never fully accepted as a consonance in the common-practice period, and there is, therefore, no conventional method for generating diatonic and/or chromatic scales with 7 as a factor comparable to those described for the three and five limits. There are, however, a large number of historical and ethnic scales embedded in the seven-limit fabric, in addition to some recently invented scales constructed along similar lines. Prominent among these are a number of seven-tone scales belonging to the three classical tetrachordal genera (diatonic, chromatic, and enharmonic). These scales, which derive primarily from Greek and Islamic sources, all share the characteristic of dividing the tetrachord (4:3) into three parts by means of superparticular ratios. Although these scales were presumably intended for modal melody and heterophony, rather than chordal harmony, some, like Ptolemy's syntonon diatonic, do include sufficient harmonic resources to be useful for chordal music.[4] Often, these scales yield more interesting harmonic possibilities when the intervals of the tetrachord are rearranged from the order specified by the ancient theorists. All of them are worthy of exploration by those wishing to discover the melodic properties of various septimal intervals. A number of the most useful seven-limit tetrachordal scales are illustrated in Figure 5.2. A thorough examination of these scales and their harmonic and melodic resources is outside the scope of this publication. Readers are encouraged to generate all of the permutations for each of these scales, to map them to a 3-D lattice such as those in Figures 5.1a and 5.1b, and to catalog their resources.

The Higher Primes: Eleven, Thirteen, and Beyond

Eleven and Thirteen

As indicated in Chapter Two, there appears to be a qualitative difference between intervals based on ratios of the integers through 8 and those based on ratios of higher numbers. This difference exists because dyads based on higher integers are not beat-free special relationships when formed from normal harmonic timbres,

Figure 5.2: Seven-limit tetrachordal scales

and because such dyads do not produce unambiguous sensations of periodicity pitch. Nevertheless, a number of composers have used intervals involving higher numbers, especially the primes 11 and 13, to good effect, and have included such intervals in their definitions of Just Intonation. Such intervals must, therefore, form a part of our discussion.

Whereas the intervals generated by 2, 3, and 5 are firmly within the realm of Western musical experience, and those based on 7 straddle the boundary between the familiar and the unknown, intervals based on 11 and 13 lie entirely outside Western musical experience. These intervals are controversial. One is likely to love or hate them on first hearing. Some composers and theorists (Harry Partch and La Monte Young, for example) hold the view that our comprehension and appreciation of musical intervals is gradually evolving up the harmonic series. From this point of view, the incorporation of 11 and 13 into our musical vocabulary constitutes the next logical step after our full acceptance and "emancipation" of 7. For the reasons alluded to above, I regard this point of view with some skepticism. If intervals of 11 and 13 have a role to play in Western, harmonic music (as distinct from modal, melodic and heterophonic music, where they definitely have a historical role) I am inclined to think it will be a subordinate one. Certainly, unless they are introduced with great care, Western listeners are more likely to hear intervals based on 11 or 13 as mere "wrong notes" than as logical extensions of our traditional harmonic vocabulary.

Whether we find intervals of 11 and 13 strange because they are not part of our traditional musical system or whether they were never incorporated into our traditional musical system because people find them strange cannot, at present, be conclusively determined. Clearly, it is the very strangeness or "otherness" of intervals of 11 or 13 that is the source of their appeal for many composers. Of course, readers should not base their judgements of the value of these intervals solely on this publication, but should listen carefully to music by composers who use such intervals and perform their own experiments in composition and ear training.

Table 5.3: Ratios of 11

Ratio	Cents
12:11	150.6
11:10	165.0
11:9	347.4
14:11	417.5
15:11	537.0
11:8	551.3
16:11	648.7
11:7	782.5
18:11	852.6
20:11	1035.0
11:6	1049.4
21:11	1119.5

PRIMARY INTERVALS

The primary interval for 11 is 11:8 (approximately 551.3 cents). This is about as far as you can get from the intervals of the twelve-tone equally tempered scale, being almost exactly the midpoint between the tempered perfect fourth and tritone. It is nearly as far removed from the intervals of five-limit diatonic Just Intonation. Some of the other intervals based on 11 fall similarly "in the cracks" relative to Western diatonic and chromatic scales. The primary interval for 13 is 13:8 (approximately 840.5 cents). This interval, while representing a less extreme departure from the familiar than 11:8, is still far enough from its simpler neighbors to defy aural classification as either a minor or major sixth. The sounds of 11:8 and 13:8 are as foreign as their cents values would indicate. Do not be misled by the fact that there are intervals that conventional music theory calls "elevenths" and "thirteenths." These intervals are merely octave extensions of tempered fourths and sixths respectively and have little in common in the way of affective properties with intervals based on the prime numbers 11 and 13.

The affective properties of 11 and 13, although quite distinctive, are very hard to describe in words, perhaps because they are entirely free of cultural associations. Trying to describe the sounds of intervals based on 11 and 13 to a person who has never heard them is about as useful as trying to describe colors to a person who has been blind from birth. I find that 11, or at least 11:8, has a sort of sneering or derisive quality that is nevertheless quite appealing in certain situations. I find 13 almost unbearably harsh, and I have had little success integrating it into my music. Ben Johnston, who has done considerable work with 11 and 13, remarks that "The eleventh partial introduces ambiguity..." (because so many 11-based intervals occupy neutral positions between more major and minor forms) and that 13 "...has a melancholy, dark quality. Nearly every time I've used it, it has something to do with death..."[5]

In addition to their respective primaries, 11 and 13, in conjunction with the lower primes, each generate a sizeable family of intervals, the simplest of which are illustrated in Tables 5.3 and 5.4. (The intervals in the tables are limited to those that involve 11 or 13 to the first power in the denominator or numerator, not multiplied

Table 5.4: Ratios of 13

Ratio	Cents
14:13	128.3
13:12	138.6
15:13	247.7
13:11	289.2
16:13	359.5
13:10	454.2
18:13	563.4
13:9	636.6
20:13	745.8
21:13	830.3
13:8	840.5
22:13	910.8
24:13	1061.4
13:7	1071.7
25:13	1132.1

by any additional, lower prime factors. If we were to include the ratios involving *multiples* of 11 and 13, that is., (22, 33, 44, ...) and (26, 39, 52, ...) the result would be a truly unwieldy collection of largely unclassifiable, and in most cases, aurally incomprehensible intervals. And that does not even consider higher *powers* of 11 and 13 and *their* multiples.) Most of the intervals of 11 and 13 have been neither named nor classified. As stated previously, only the simplest of these intervals, such as 11:6, 11:8, and 13:8, can make even a remote claim of consonance, and that only in special circumstances.

Some of the intervals of 11 have been described as *neutral* intervals, because they fall almost exactly between familiar major and minor intervals, not because they are in any sense lacking in affective power. These include two neutral seconds, 12:11 (150.6 cents) and 11:10 (165 cents); a neutral third, 11:9 (347.4 cents); a neutral sixth, 18:11 (852.6 cents); and a neutral seventh, 11:6 (1049.4 cents). In addition, 11:8 (551.3 cents) and its complement 16:11 (648.7 cents) might be considered "neutral tritones." As is evident from their cents values, these neutral ratios of 11 are very closely approximated in twenty-four-tone equal temperament (the "quarter-tone scale"). Some of the intervals of 13, such as 15:13, 16:13, and 13:10, could also be considered neutral, although they do not fall as neatly "in the cracks" as do the intervals of 11. The remaining intervals of 11 and 13 are not easily categorized.

At least one group of multiple-number intervals involving 11 and/or 13 deserves special attention. These are the microtones illustrated in Table 5.5. These intervals, all superparticular, might prove useful for harmonic voice leading in a chordal music incorporating 11 and 13. Two of these intervals, 33:32 and 65:64 correspond to the symbols used in Ben Johnston's notation system, used in this publication, to designate inflection by 11 and 13, respectively.

CHORDS AND HARMONY

The problem of systematically integrating intervals involving 11 and/or 13 into a Western-style harmonic system along with intervals based on 2, 3, 5, and 7 is a formidable one. Although some composers have attempted this, it remains an open question whether music involving these intervals will ever meet with wide acceptance. Harry Partch based his musical system on hexads, chords of six notes with the relative frequencies 4:5:6:7:9:11, representing identities 1-5-3-7-9-11 (in other words, a dominant-ninth chord with an added harmonic eleventh).[6] In the case of a chord based on $1/1$, the tones would be $1/1$, $5/4$, $3/2$, $7/4$, $9/8$, and $11/8$. (Because of the difficulty of representing a four or greater dimensional lattice on a two dimensional surface, we will not offer lattice representations of chords involving higher primes.) In root position and in a reasonably high register, the addition of the 11 identity to the dominant-ninth chord doesn't seriously injure its stability or consonance, although it does add an indescribable, piquant quality to the sonority. It should also be observed that adding the 11 identity adds a second tritone, 11:8 (or its octave extension 11:4) to the chord, and may thereby contribute some additional tension.

From Partch's hexad, it is a small step to add the 13 identity and make a *heptad* or *septad*, that is, a chord with the relative frequencies 4:5:6:7:9:11:*13*, and some of Partch's successors have done so. Again, in root position this is an acceptable enough chord, albeit with yet more added "bite" from the 13 identity. The 13 identity adds yet another tritone, 13:9 (636.6 cents), to the chord. The effect of the added 11 and 13 identities, and the effect of subsequent higher prime identities in general depends, to a significant extent, on the timbre being used. We

Table 5.5: Eleven- and thirteen-limit microtones

Ratio	Factors	Cents
22:21	$(2 \times 11):(3 \times 7)$	80.5
33:32	$(3 \times 11):2^5$	53.3
40:39	$(2^3 \times 5):(3 \times 13)$	43.8
45:44	$(3^2 \times 5):(2^2 \times 11)$	38.9
55:54	$(5 \times 11):(2 \times 3^3)$	31.8
56:55	$(2^3 \times 7):(5 \times 11)$	31.2
65:64	$(5 \times 13):2^6$	26.8
66:65	$(2 \times 3 \times 11):(5 \times 13)$	26.4
78:77	$(2 \times 3 \times 13):(7 \times 11)$	22.3

are accustomed to hearing timbres in music in which the harmonics at least through 16 make a significant contribution. Hence adding an 11 and/or 13 identity on top of a stable, root-position dominant-ninth chord will not create much of a disturbance, provided that the tones being used for the higher identities are of fairly simple composition. If the higher identities are represented by tones with many strong harmonics, however, the effect is likely to be quite harsh.

Of course, harmonic music in the West does not generally consist of six- or seven-voice chords in root position, moving in parallel. (One can, of course, use these chords in exactly that way, that is, in the manner of the French impressionists; many novel sonorities might be developed by using 11 and 13, or higher primes, the only obvious penalty being the requirement of a rather large number of different pitches.) The application of chords including higher prime identities to a more traditional, Western style of harmonic or polyphonic music, where three or four distinct voices constitute the norm and in which contrary motion and smooth voice leading are highly valued, presents far greater difficulties. These difficulties arise in part from the great variety of resources offered by the inclusion of higher primes. From the tones of the harmonic heptad, it is possible to extract twenty-five different triadic subsets that include an 11 and/or 13 identity (ten with 11 only, ten with 13 only, and five with both). In addition, the harmonic heptad includes thirty different tetrads, twenty different pentads, and six different hexads that include 11 and/or 13. (If subharmonic materials are included, the number of possibilities doubles.) If one chooses to admit the next higher nonprime odd-number identity, 15, as some composers are wont to do, the situation becomes even more complex. And these are merely the resources provided by a *single* harmonic heptad. When extended to a tonal fabric of four or five dimensions, the variety of possibilities, both harmonic and melodic, becomes truly overwhelming.

What are the moods of these various combinations? How do they sound in close or spread voicings? Which identities are best doubled and which can be omitted in textures where full hexads or heptads are unsuitable? What "tendencies" do they have for movement to other tonalities? At present, the answers to most of these questions remain unknown and are unlikely to be discovered except through extensive compositional practice and experimentation. To attain a full mastery of these complex materials is a task that could easily consume a lifetime (or several lifetimes) of ear training, composition, and analysis. The task is made more challenging, but also potentially more rewarding, by the near-total absence of any traditional models for the harmonic or polyphonic use of these higher primes.

Of course, some generalizations can be made. As is the case with lower prime limits, the most consonant and stable chords are those that follow the model of the harmonic series, with low identities and wider spacings at the bottom and higher identities and narrower spacings at the top. The consonance of chords with higher identities can also be enhanced by using voicings or inversions that avoid clusters of consecutive harmonics above 7 or 8, for example, use 4:5:6:7:9:11 rather than 7:8:9:10:11:12. Of course, if maximum "bite" is the desired effect, clusters of consecutive harmonics from 8 through 16 certainly have the ability to provide it. In general, chords that lack the lower identities, especially 1 and 3, are more likely to be perceived as ambiguous in tonal meaning, as are voicings and inversions that place high prime identities in the bass voice. Beyond these simple guidelines, the applications and characteristics of chords involving the 11 and 13 identities remain to be discovered.

To some extent, the difficulties of composing harmonic music based on the eleven or thirteen limit may result not from any special characteristics of the intervals of 11 or 13, but from the simple fact of having six or seven different identities in a chord. Information theory holds that the untrained observer can recognize approximately 7 ± 2 different stimuli that vary in only one parameter.[7] This finding is often cited to account for the wide distribution of pentatonic and heptatonic scales. From this perspective, a single hexad or heptad may contain nearly as much information as a casual listener can easily grasp. Thus, a music in which hexads or heptads are built on a great many different roots may easily exceed the information processing capacities of all but the most acute listeners, regardless of the psychoacoustic properties of the particular tonalities. Hence, we might want to postulate a tentative rule: the greater the number of identities admitted in the tonalities in a given music, the fewer tonal roots should be used in order to avoid disorientation resulting from information overload. The reduction in the number of available harmonic roots need not make the resulting harmonic texture static. If the music is based on a predominantly three- or four-voiced texture, it is quite possible for apparent harmonic motion to occur within the confines of a single tonality, with tension being produced by movement from low to high identities and resolution being produced by the opposite motion.

For the composer who is interested in experimenting with the resources provided by 11 and/or 13, but who is not prepared to cope with the complexities described above, there are a number of possible approaches for reducing the complexity to a manageable level. One possibility is to select a subset of the available identities within a given limit and work only with those identities in a given movement or composition. The primes through 13 include twelve groups of four primes, sixteen groups of three primes, and nine groups of two primes, all including an 11 or 13 identity. It would be possible to use any one of these subsets as a basis for composition, although those involving 2 and 3 are likely to be most easily handled, since they include the familiar perfect fourth and perfect fifth, which can serve as orienting devices.

A number of composers and theorists have either created fixed tonal sets that explicitly include intervals based on 11 and/or 13, or have developed methods of pitch-set generation that are independent of prime limit but are readily applicable to intervals based on higher primes. Among these are Harry Partch's tonality diamond,[8] Ben Johnston's ratio scales,[9] Ervin Wilson's combination product sets,[10, 11] and John Chalmers's tritriadic scales.[12] A discussion of these structures is beyond the scope of this publication; interested readers should consult the reference notes for this chapter for information.

SEVENTEEN AND NINETEEN

Whereas 11 and 13 are about as far removed as possible from Western musical practice, the next two primes, 17 and nineteen, bring us back to more familiar territory. The primary interval for 17, 17:16 (105.0 cents) is very close to a tempered semitone and the defect of this interval from a 9:8 major whole tone, 18:17, is even closer at approximately 99.0 cents. Indeed, Vincenzo Galilei, the father of Galileo, specified a measurement of 18:17 for placing successive frets on the lute, as a "quick and dirty" approximation for equal temperament.[13] Since $18^{12}:17^{12}$ is approximately 1187.5 cents, 12.5 cents short of an octave, the lutenist presumably "fudged" the positions of the frets, rather than strictly obeying Galilei's measurements. The primary interval for nineteen, 19:16 (297.5 cents), is very close to the tempered minor third. Being so close to familiar tempered intervals, these ratios of 17 and nineteen are readily accepted by Western listeners, but may or may not have any substantial contribution to make to the expansion of tonality in Just Intonation.

The number 17 is a constituent of the tuning proposed by Alexander Ellis for the diminished-seventh chord: 10:12:14:17.[14] Ellis remarks that this chord is smoother than either the tempered or five-limit version of the diminished seventh, an observation which my own experience confirms, but also indicates that the existence of the diminished seventh chord is really a consequence of temperament. Adding the fundamental of the harmonic series below the diminished-seventh chord yields a chord with the relative frequencies 8:10:12:14:17 in root position—a dominant-minor-ninth chord. (This is consistent with the conventional explanation of the diminished-seventh chord as a dominant minor-ninth chord with a missing root.) Ward Widener, an electronic engineer and designer of electronic tuning machines, advocates two additional chord tunings involving 17: 10:12:15:17 and 12:15:17:21.[15] The former he considers a minor-sixth chord, that is, a minor triad with an added major second. It can be regarded as a chromatic alteration of the more common five-limit minor-seventh chord, 10:12:15:18. The latter is a variety of the 7♭5 chord. Various other combinations and subsets of the dominant-minor-ninth chord and of Widener's chords, such as 12:15:17, 8:10:12:15:17, and 12:14:17:21 also seem to have some potential value as condissonant chords.

The number 17 is also a constituent of one tuning of La Monte Young's "Dream Chords," used in various "Dream" compositions, such as *The Four Dreams of China*, *The Subsequent Dreams of China*, and *The Second Dream of the High Tension Line Step-Down Transformer*. The Dream Chord consists of the three-limit triad 6:8:9, with an additional tone dividing the 9:8. Young has used various divisions over the years, including 36:35:32 (9:8 = 36:32) and 63:62:56 (9:8 = 63:56), but he currently favors the 18:17:16 division (18:16 = 9:8), the only possible division consisting of consecutive harmonics.

The interval 19:16 has been proposed as a tuning for the minor third in the minor triad, yielding a chord with the relative frequencies 16:19:24. As its advocates point out, this tuning causes the nominal root of the chord to coincide with fundamental of the harmonic series from which it derives, a property that is lacking in the more consonant minor triads from the five and seven limits, 10:12:15 and 6:7:9. However, 19:16 is definitely not a consonance, no more so than is the tempered minor third, and therefore does not yield a consonant triad. In any case, it appears that a group of tones with relative frequencies higher than 8 or 9 is likely to produce an ambiguous sensation of periodicity pitch, so that nothing of practical value is achieved by making the root of the chord the fundamental of the harmonic series. Nineteen also figures in a proposed tuning for the augmented triad: 12:15:19. The augmented triad is traditionally considered a discord and this chord certainly fits that description, although it is not apparent that it is any better than the more complex five-limit version 16:20:25. Ward Widener also proposes several chord tunings involving nineteen: 10:12:14:19, for a diminished major-seventh chord; 10:12:15:19, for a minor-major-seventh chord; and 12:15:19:21 for a 7♯5 chord. Although these tunings appear to represent the lowest-numbered harmonic-series segments compatible with the respective chord types, all of these chromatically altered chords came into being under the influence of equal temperament and their usefulness in Just Intonation is far from self-evident.

BEYOND NINETEEN

In recent years, a few composers have worked with tunings based on prime numbers above 19. In the 1980s Glenn Branca composed several "symphonies" for large ensembles of modified electric guitars and other stringed instruments playing a tuning based on the harmonics through 128, often at extreme volumes. Although there is a kind of cohesion due to all of the tones being harmonics of a single fundamental, and harmonic motion can sometimes be detected, the overall effect of this music is more of a dense "wall of sound" (quite beyond any that Phil Spector ever produced) and a relentlessly hammering rhythm than of anything normally identified as harmony.

La Monte Young has long been interested in the effects of higher primes. I have already mentioned his use of the primes 17 and 31 in the division of the 9:8 interval in his "Dream Chord." In 1967, Young composed a piece entitled *5 V 67 6:38 PM NYC*, which used all of the harmonics in the segment 56–72 except those that are multiples of 5. These harmonics form a pair of 9:8s separated by a central 64:63, a structure that is present in the tuning of *The Well-Tuned Piano*, and which Young likens to a pair of "micro-tetrachords." The resulting series is 56:57:58:59:61:62:63:64:66:67: 68:69:71:72, the two 9:8s being delineated by 56:63 and 64:72. This series contains the primes 59, 61, 67, and 71, in addition to octave doubles of 29 and 31. In 1989, Young composed *The Romantic Symmetry in Prime Time from 112 to 144 with 119*, which utilizes primes and octave multiples of primes which fall in the harmonic-series segment 112–144 (an octave transposition of 56–72), plus the nonprime 119 (7 × 17). This piece was originally presented as a continuous sound environment, the pitches being generated by the extremely precise Rayna Synthesizer. Later, Young produced a "big band" realization of the piece, entitled *The Lower Map of The Eleven's Division in The Romantic Symmetry (over a 60 cycle base) in Prime Time from 122 to 119 with 144*. In this piece, a large ensemble of brass, electric guitars and basses, and four vocalists play along with the electronically generated sound environment. The musicians play selected frequencies from the series 8:14:16:29:31:59:61. In addition to the pitches the musicians can play, the broad time structure of the piece is strictly specified, but the entries and exits of individual players are improvised according to a set of rules, as is typical of many of Young's compositions. The resulting sound is rich and complex, and potentially absorbing if one comes to it with the proper mind set, but it is debatable whether the properties of the sound are in any detectable way a product of the precise frequency ratios used. Young admits that neither he nor any of his musicians can produce the precise pitches required by the piece without the support of the sound environment, and there is certainly no evidence in any of the psychoacoustic literature that I have examined that anyone could hope to do so in the foreseeable future. Young disputes the view expressed above, and I must confess that my view of the piece is based on only a single hearing of a recorded version, and certainly cannot be considered definitive. In 1993, Young opened a sound environment based on a "symmetry" using harmonics from the 224–288 segment.

It is interesting to note that both Young's and Branca's work involving higher harmonics is harmonically static, that is, there is no "root movement," or change of chord or key. It may be that, for the foreseeable future, the only way listeners stand a chance of comprehending these higher identities is in the context of such static structures.

PRACTICAL JUST INTONATION WITH REAL INSTRUMENTS

INTRODUCTION

Obviously, all of the information in the previous chapters of this publication is useless if it does not result in music being composed, performed, recorded, and heard. There are a number of possible approaches to obtaining practical Just Intonation, each of which offers distinct advantages and disadvantages. The principal approaches are:

✔ Building original instruments

✔ Using those conventional instruments that have no intonational restrictions, such as unfretted strings, trombone, voice

✔ Retuning or modifying conventional instruments and/ or playing them with unconventional techniques

✔ Using computers and synthesizers

The first approach, building original instruments, is well known as a result of the work of Just Intonation pioneers Harry Partch and Lou Harrison, and, in the minds of some who first encountered Just Intonation through the works of these two composers, the two ideas may be inextricably bound. Up until the appearance of affordable synthesizers with user-programmable tuning capabilities in the late 1970s and early 1980s, this was probably the most common method for obtaining Just Intonation. The disadvantages of building original instruments are obvious. It is an activity that requires considerable skill, and consumes time, space, and money. For the person who overcomes these obstacles and produces a workable instrument, there next surfaces the difficulty of learning to play the result or finding someone who is willing to do so. Then there is the further problem that if you base your compositions on novel instruments of which you possess the only examples, the only performances of your works will be those that you organize. Hence, you will have saddled yourself with the jobs of instrument builder, repair person, music director/conductor, and manager, in addition to composer and performer. This is a lot of work for one person, especially if he or she also has to practice some other trade in order to survive.[1]

On the positive side, instrument building places another aspect of music under the direct control of the composer. It can also provide valuable lessons in musical acoustics, a topic about which no composer interested in tuning can afford to be ignorant. Further, the experience of conceiving a new instrument and successfully bringing it into existence can give considerable satisfaction in its own right. Lou Harrison calls it "one of music's greatest joys."[2] And, as those who are familiar with the music of Harry Partch or the gamelan music of Lou Harrison will attest, the timbres as well as the tunings of these composers' instruments are an indispensable part of their music.

Where continuous-pitch instruments and the voice are concerned, the obvious advantage is that instruments, and players and singers with high levels of skill and musicality, are readily available. The principal disadvantage is that few players or singers understand Just Intonation or have been trained to produce it. Further, players and singers, as a result of their training and experience, may have developed definite ideas as to what constitutes "good" intonation and may be resistant or even hostile to change. The approach of retuning conventional instruments and/or using alternative playing techniques offers essentially the same advantages and disadvantages as using continuous-pitch instruments: instruments and skilled players abound, but few players have acquired the skills necessary to play their instruments in Just Intonation, and many may be resistant to doing so. Lou Harrison has pointed out that many orchestras consider the retuning of their pianos to an alternate tuning to be something on the order of sacrilege. Hence, getting a satisfactory performance with conventional instruments, continuous pitch or otherwise, requires finding performers with the proper attitude. This may prove quite difficult, and a young and/or unknown composer pursuing this course may get even fewer performances than the builder of novel instruments.

Given the difficulties presented by the approaches described above, it is not surprising that electronic instruments with user-programmable tuning capabilities have received considerable attention from composers interested in alternate tunings, especially those who came of age in the 1970s and 1980s. The advantages presented by these instruments are numerous. Any desired tuning within the instrument's precision can be created and stored in the instrument's memory and/or saved to disk for later recall. In many cases, several tunings can be stored and switched among instantaneously under program control, making modulation and transposition of complex just tonal structures entirely practical. The cost of a modest MIDI studio is no more than that of a decent used car, and a truly lavish setup is still likely to cost less than a good grand piano. With such equipment, a composer can control every aspect of the production of his or her work.

On the negative side, the expressive properties of electronic instruments, while greatly improved over the past few years, have some way to go before they can match those of traditional acoustic instruments. And the timbres of digital instruments, even those that use samples of acoustic sounds, cannot, as yet, match the richness and variety of those produced by acoustic instruments. Another problem is that the tuning resolution of instruments that offer alternate tuning capabilities is often less than a serious devotee of Just Intonation might desire. The best commercial instruments available at the time of this writing offer a resolution of 1024 steps per octave, equivalent to a minimum step size of 1.17 cents, or a maximum error of 0.59 cents. This, though far from ideal, is acceptable for most purposes, and is probably as accurate as any tuning one is likely to obtain with acoustic instruments under practical playing conditions. However, some less expensive instruments have coarser resolutions, and even some of the best have resolutions that are constant in Hz rather than cents, so that the upper and middle registers offer more than adequate resolution while the bass resolution may be quite poor.

In this chapter, we will explore three of the four approaches enumerated above. The building of original instruments will not be addressed here, as the possibilities are so vast as to require a book in their own right, if not several. Readers interested in this topic should consult Partch's *Genesis of a Music* and the periodical *Experimental Musical Instruments*.[3] In the seventeen years that I have been working with Just Intonation, I have yet to see an original acoustic instrument with sufficient pitch precision for playing in Just Intonation that did not belong to one of the families described below, so the material that follows should be of some interest to would-be instrument builders. The chapter will conclude with some thoughts on how to obtain satisfactory performances in Just Intonation with conventional instruments.

FIXED-PITCH INSTRUMENTS

ACOUSTIC KEYBOARDS

Most keyboard instruments can be retuned with more or less effort to some form of fixed-scale Just Intonation. The amount of skill required for such retuning varies considerably, depending on the instrument and the tuning. Harpsichords and clavichords (the unfretted type, with a separate string for each note) are probably the easiest. Harpsichordists and clavichordists who are involved in authentic performance of early music presumably already have the necessary skills, at least for five-limit tunings.

PIANO PROBLEMS

Pianos are more difficult to retune because of the greater inharmonicity of their strings and because they are equipped with three strings per note in the treble range and two strings per note over most of the bass range. It is, of course, impossible to keep three strings tuned in a perfect unison for any appreciable period. In practice, however, piano tuners do not normally even attempt such a unison. The strings for a given note on a piano are typically detuned over a range of from 2 to 8 cents. This detuning is part of the characteristic sound of the piano. It not only adds a chorus effect to the timbre of the instrument, but also has a significant effect on the amplitude envelope of the sound. Because the two or three strings of a piano tone are not perfectly in tune, their phase relationship is in a state of constant variation. Hence, when one string is pushing down on the bridge, another may be pulling up. Energy is cyclically transferred from the strings to the bridge and back to the strings. As a result, the transfer of energy from the strings to the bridge and soundboard is considerably slower than for an instrument with only one string per note, and the decay time of the tone is lengthened accordingly.

Most Just Intonation pianists avoid the tuning problems produced by multiple strings by using only a single string per note. They either remove the additional strings, damp them using tuner's mutes ("tempering strips"), or modify the action so that the *una corda* pedal causes the hammers to strike only a single string per course. A single-strung piano has a sound that is quite distinct from that of a normal instrument, as can be readily confirmed by listening to a recording made on such an instrument, such as La Monte Young's *The Well-Tuned Piano* or Michael Harrison's *From Ancient Worlds*. The timbre is more string-like in character than that of a normal piano, with a more incisive attack, somewhat akin to the tone of a hammered dulcimer.

Although the problems created by multiple strings are easily solved, those resulting from inharmonicity are inherent in the structure of the instrument. As stated in Chapter 2, all impulsively excited (plucked or struck) strings produce tones with partials that deviate to some extent from the harmonic series of the fundamental. In most musical strings, the inharmonicity is insufficient to have any detectable influence on tuning. However, on instruments which have particularly stiff strings, such as the piano, the inharmonicity is considerable and special tuning techniques are necessary to compensate for it.

A perfectly uniform and perfectly elastic would string produce tones with perfectly harmonic partials. Unfortunately, this kind of string exists only in the imaginations of physicists. Stiffness causes real strings to behave in a manner that is a composite of the behavior of an ideal string and that of a bar or rod that is hinged at both ends. A hinged bar has partials with frequencies that are the *squares* of integer multiples of the fundamental (for example, f, $2f^2$, $3f^2$, …). The effect of this "barlike" component makes the frequencies of the partials of real strings higher than those of the ideal string described above. In particular, the effect is to make each successive partial of the real string deviate *further* from the harmonic ideal than the previous one. The degree of inharmonicity depends on the length, diameter, and tension of the string relative to its stiffness. The longer, thinner, and tauter a string is, the closer its partials will be to true harmonics.

Unfortunately, because there is a practical limit to the length of a piano, it is impossible to use the long and thin strings that might otherwise be desirable. And it will not do to simply thicken and shorten the strings to obtain the desired pitches. The thickened strings would possess far too much of the barlike component and would sound more like chimes in a cheap clock than strings. Hence the usual procedure is to wind the lower strings with copper wire, which adds mass and therefore lowers the frequency, without increasing stiffness to unacceptable levels. Nevertheless, there are limits to how short a piano can be made while avoiding an unacceptable amount of inharmonicity in the bass register. All other factors being equal, the longer a piano is, the better for both intonation and tone.

Table 6.1: Piano-String Partials vs. True Harmonics

Mode #	Harmonic Series (Hz)	Harmonic Series (Cents)	Piano String (Hz)	Piano String (Cents)	Deviation (Cents)
1	261.63	0.0	261.63	0.0	0.0
2	523.26	1200.0	523.51	1200.8	0.8
3	784.89	1901.9	785.91	1904.2	2.3
4	1046.52	2400.0	1049.23	2404.5	4.5
5	1308.15	2786.3	1313.30	2793.1	6.8
6	1569.78	3101.9	1578.68	3111.7	9.8

Table 6.1 shows the frequencies of the first six partials of a typical grand piano string tuned to middle C compared to the first six degrees of a true harmonic series based on the same fundamental.[4] It is evident from the table that the deviation of the string's partials from the harmonic series increases with the partial number, reaching nearly 10 cents at the sixth partial. Above middle C the degree of inharmonicity increases by a factor of approximately 2.67 for each octave, whereas below middle C, the inharmonicity decreases by the same amount until the wound bass strings are reached.[5] The increase in inharmonicity with rising pitch is a result of the fact that stiffness plays an increasing role in string behavior as the strings are shortened. It is impossible to fully compensate for this factor by either increasing tension or reducing string thickness. Either of these approaches can result in string breakage, and thinning the string excessively will also result in it having insufficient power to drive the soundboard effectively.

The consequence of the piano's inharmonicity is that it is impossible to tune a simple-ratio interval by "zero beating" its defining pair of partials. Consider a pair of such strings with the same degree of inharmonicity, but with fundamentals related by a perfect fifth. If one were to tune the strings so that the second partial of the higher string perfectly matched the third partial of the lower string, the fourth and sixth partials of the respective strings would be mismatched and beat at a rate of 3.52Hz (Table 6.2a). If the tuning is adjusted to bring the fourth and sixth partials into unison, the second and third will beat at a rate of 1.75Hz (Table 6.2b). In neither of the above cases are the fundamentals of the two strings in a perfect 3:2 ratio. If we tune the fundamentals to this ideal ratio (which could only be done with the aid of a monochord or an electronic tuner) both pairs of partials will beat, at rates of 0.64 and 4.83Hz respectively (Table 6.2c). In actual practice, the matter is even more complicated, as altering the tension of the string also shifts the frequencies of the partials somewhat. While there is no absolute agreement, the most common practice among those tuning pianos in Just Intonation appears to be to tune the most important intervals to produce the least overall beating or maximum smoothness. It is not too difficult, in the case of our perfect fifth, above, to achieve an acceptable compromise, but keep in mind that for intervals involving higher pairs of defining partials, the deviation will be greater, as will that for the same interval in a higher octave. It should also be noted that "the most important intervals" in a given tuning may not necessarily be the primary intervals that define the tuning as viewed on the lattice, but rather those that feature most prominently in a particular composition. The practice described above derives primarily from those tuning pianos for solo performance. The problem of tuning a piano in Just Intonation for use with an ensemble of instruments most of which produce harmonic partials might require a different solution, but I was not able to obtain any practical information on this question, and it seems unlikely that the matter has been adequately examined.

Although piano tunings produced by the compromise method described above do not conform strictly to the definition of Just Intonation as "any tuning in which all of the intervals can be represented by whole-number ratios," they operate on the analogous aesthetic principle of using the smoothest available tunings for consonant intervals and produce a similar aesthetic effect to that of true simple-ratio intervals played on instruments that produce harmonic partials. A number of artists have successfully tuned pianos in Just Intonation, at least through the seven limit, and have developed successful compositions for solo performance. The best known of these are La Monte Young, Terry Riley, and Michael Harrison. In addition, Lou Harrison has used retuned piano in a number of pieces for both large and small ensembles, including a *Concerto for Piano with Javanese Gamelan* and a *Concerto for Piano with Selected Orchestra*.

If you're going to experiment on a piano of reasonable quality (which is the only kind likely to produce results worth the effort), it might be a good idea to take some lessons from a professional tuner. It is one thing to recognize when an interval has achieved a state of minimum beating, and quite another to be able to manipulate the tuning pins of a piano quickly and efficiently to achieve this result and have it remain relatively stable under playing conditions. Further, some tuners claim

Table 6.2: Three possible tunings of a perfect fifth on typical piano strings

	A.			
String 1		**String 2**		
Partial	Hz	Partial	Hz	f_B
1	261.63	—	—	—
—	—	1	392.76	—
2	523.51	—	—	—
3	785.91	2	785.91	0.0
4	1049.23	—	—	—
—	—	3	1179.81	—
5	1313.30	—	—	—
6	1578.68	4	1575.16	3.52
	B.			
String 1		**String 2**		
Partial	Hz	Partial	Hz	f_B
1	261.63	—	—	—
—	—	1	393.64	—
2	523.51	—	—	—
3	785.91	2	787.66	1.75
4	1049.23	—	—	—
—	—	3	1182.44	—
5	1313.30	—	—	—
6	1578.68	4	1578.68	0.0
	C.			
String 1		**String 2**		
Partial	Hz	Partial	Hz	f_B
1	261.63	—	—	—
—	—	1	391.5	—
2	523.51	—	—	—
3	785.91	2	785.27	0.64
4	1049.23	—	—	—
—	—	3	1178.87	—
5	1313.30	—	—	—
6	1578.68	4	1573.85	4.83

that improper tuning technique can damage a piano so it will not hold a tuning. Because of the limited range of tensions a string will tolerate without breaking, on the one hand, or producing an unsatisfactory tone, on the other, all stringed keyboards should probably be limited to tunings of twelve tones-per-octave. This does not mean, however, that one must use *the same* twelve tones in every octave. For example, the tuning of Ben Johnston's *Sonata for Microtonal Piano* (1962) uses eighty-one different pitches; only seven pitches have octave duplicates.

REED ORGANS

Reed organs were favorites of Harry Partch, and of nineteenth-century experimenters such as Bosanquet, Colin Brown, Helmholtz, and Ellis, but such of these instruments that still survive are likely to be expensive antiques and hence probably not suitable candidates for retuning. Reed organs do have an advantage over stringed keyboard instruments in that they are not limited to twelve tones per octave. Partch's "Chromelodeons" (retuned reed organs) embodied his complete 43-tone tuning. Another advantage offered by reed organs over stringed keyboards is that they produce true harmonic partials and hence provide the maximum definition for just intervals, desirable both for tuning accuracy and aesthetic appreciation. The basic principle for tuning a free reed of the type used in reed organs is to remove material from the tip (reducing mass and hence increasing frequency of vibration) to raise pitch or from the base (reducing stiffness and hence lowering frequency of vibration) to lower pitch. This method is also applicable to accordions and, potentially, to harmonicas, although I am not aware of anyone having retuned a harmonica. Pauline Oliveros has, in recent years, been performing on a justly tuned accordion. For more detailed instructions on retuning reed organs, see Harry Partch's *Genesis of a Music*.

PIPE ORGANS

Although few of us are likely to have the opportunity to retune a pipe organ, these too are potentially retunable in Just Intonation. Most organ pipes are equipped with movable stoppers or collars that adjust their effective sounding lengths. Organ pipes produce true harmonic partials and are hence easy to tune to simple-ratio intervals. Open pipes, which produce a full complement of harmonics, are easier to tune than stopped pipes, which produce only odd-numbered harmonics. Different stops can be given different tunings and multiple manuals can be used to facilitate movement from one tuning to another.

ELECTROACOUSTIC KEYBOARDS

Among electroacoustic keyboards, the Hohner Clavinet and Fender Rhodes Electric Piano are good candidates for retuning. These instruments are especially suitable for experimentation because inexpensive synthesizers have largely usurped their roles in pop music, making used instruments available at very reasonable prices. The Clavinet is a stringed instrument, essentially an amplified clavichord. Its tuning mechanism is operated by screws that are easily accessible behind the front panel of the instrument. The strings are normally under low tension and can easily be retuned by 200 cents with little likelihood of breakage. The Rhodes piano uses metal tines for tone production. Each tine is encircled by a small spring, which can be repositioned to alter the tuning of the tine. Moving the spring toward the free end of the tine lowers the pitch; moving the spring toward the base of the tine raises the pitch. Note, however, that the Rhodes piano is essentially an ideophone, and produces tones lacking in harmonic partials. See the discussion on ideophones, below, for factors affecting the suitability of ideophones for Just Intonation.

ELECTRONIC ORGANS

Among electronic organs, those older models that use separate oscillators for each tone of the octave are practical for retuning, usually by means of slug-tuned inductors. Terry Riley performed extensively on such instruments in the 1970s. Organs with integrated top-octave generators are not retunable except by means of added circuitry which is beyond the scope of this article (and which, in the age of inexpensive retunable synthesizers, is probably not worth the trouble).

Regardless of what instrument is being retuned, some kind of tuning reference will be extremely useful, whether it be a computer or synthesizer that can generate tones of known frequency, a strobe tuner, or in the absence of more high-tech devices, a monochord.

STRINGED INSTRUMENTS WITH ONE STRING PER NOTE

The case of one-string-per-note instruments, for example, harps, psalteries, zithers, and the like, is much the same as that of the stringed keyboard instruments. Although all of these instruments have some string inharmonicity, none are as problematic as the piano. Because of limitations on string tension, they are generally limited to the number of tones per octave for which they were originally designed, but within those limits they are adaptable to whatever scheme of intonation one might devise. Of course, the pedals of the modern concert harp, which shift the pitch of groups of strings by tempered semitones, are of no use for just compositions. Of special interest are psalteries of the East-Asian style that feature movable bridges, for example, the Japanese *koto*, the Chinese *cheng*, and the like. These instruments are far more flexible of intonation than their western counterparts, since the effective sounding lengths of the strings can be easily varied. In addition, pitch can be raised by pressing on the string behind the movable bridge. With harps and psalteries, it is well to remember that, as with the keyboards, it is by no means mandatory to tune exactly the same sequence of tones in every octave.

FRETTED INSTRUMENTS

As mentioned in the introduction, some historical sources indicate that fretted instruments (lutes and viols) were the first instruments to be regularly tuned in equal temperament, having preceded keyboards in this respect by about 150 years. The reason for this is that equal temperament allows straight frets to produce useful notes on every string. Just Intonation in more than a few closely related keys demands either very closely spaced frets, or else frets that do not go straight across the neck but rather "jog" to make comma adjustments for different strings. Nevertheless, Just Intonation on fretted instruments is possible. Over the last 150 years, a variety of systems of movable frets and interchangeable fingerboards have been developed, primarily for the guitar.[6] One of the earliest of these was produced by the British experimenter General Perronet Thompson, who also worked with reed organs and may well have coined the term "Just Intonation," circa 1829. Harry Partch experimented with refretting guitars, but generally seems to have preferred unfretted, steel-guitar-type instruments over complex schemes of fixed frets. Instruments of this type are more properly classified as "continuous pitch instruments." The best known guitars with interchangeable fretboards are those that were produced by classical guitarist Tom Stone in the 1970s and 80s, under the tradenames "Intonation Systems" and "Novatone." The Intonation Systems guitars used an aluminum channel to hold the fretboards, and proved unreliable in the long run. The Novatone fretboards, which were held in place by a magnetic plastic material, were more successful, but not successful enough to keep Novatone in business. Today, they are occasionally available in kit form.[7] A more recent development that looks promising is a system developed by a German luthier named Walter Vogt. Vogt's system provides separate, adjustable frets on each string. These frets slide in tracks cut in the fingerboard, and are held in place by rubber o-rings. Unfortunately, Vogt died in 1991, and the future commercial availability of his system is uncertain at the present time.[8]

Figure 6.1: Tying a fret knot

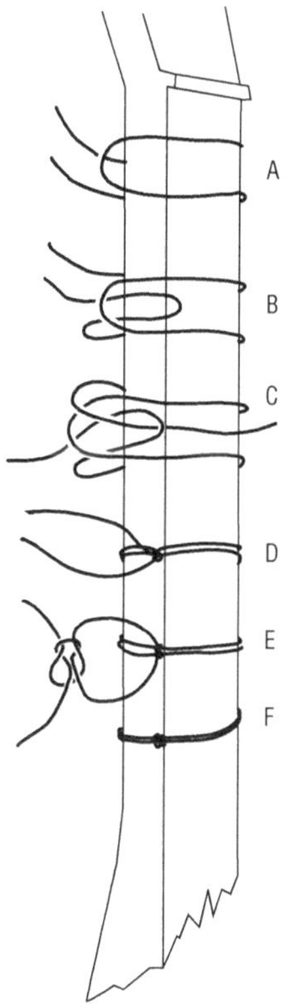

Some guitars have been made with extensive just gamuts on fixed fretboards, for example that of David Canright, which has 52 frets total, 38 of which are in the first octave, but instruments of this type are generally extremely difficult to play.

For the casual experimenter, frets of monofilament nylon may prove useful. These frets are tied around the guitar neck using the technique in Figure 6.1. (Tied frets made of gut were once the norm for lutes and viols; they remain in use in many nonindustrial societies.) A cheap guitar (electric or acoustic) can be quickly and easily modified by the removal of the original frets and their replacement with tied nylon frets. The placement of frets as close together as a syntonic comma near the nut is not out of the question, especially on long-scale instruments, though, of course, wider spacings make for easier playing.

Although the discussion above is concerned mostly with guitars, it applies equally to other fretted instruments. And one should not forget that frets, though presently associated mostly with plucked strings, can also be used with bowed stringed instruments. The instruments of the viol family, popular in the Renaissance and early baroque as both solo and ensemble instruments, were equipped with frets. There is no reason why this practice could not be revived to aid in the production of Just Intonation on bowed strings.

Table 6.3: The first four partials of a rectangular bar

Mode #	Relative Frequency	Cents
1	1.00	0.00
2	2.68	1,706.67
3	3.73	2,279.00
4	5.25	2,870.77

IDIOPHONES

The instruments classified by musicologists as ideophones, which are characterized by the use of resonant bodies of elastic materials such as metal or wood, usually in the form of bars, rods, or plates, occupy a unique position with regard to intonation, because such bodies produce partials that are totally inharmonic. Table 6.3, for example, shows the relative frequencies of the first four partials of a freely suspended uniform rectangular bar, such as might be used as a metallophone or marimba key.[9] At first glance, this would seem to render these instruments unsuitable for Just Intonation, given the important role played by harmonic partials in defining simple-ratio intervals. However, on examining the body of works composed for Just Intonation in the U.S. during the last century, one cannot avoid noticing that these instruments have played quite a prominent role. This tendency began with the late Harry Partch, who, during the 1940s, '50s, and '60s, built a large ensemble of instruments, of which at least half were ideophones. Partch's ensemble included hardwood and softwood marimbas covering a great part of the audible range, bamboo marimbas, bell-like pyrex glass "cloud-chamber bowls," and a miscellany of unique instruments using unconventional materials such as liquor bottles, lightbulbs, hubcaps, and brass artillery-shell casings.[10] What Partch did for wood and bamboo, Lou Harrison has done for metal. Beginning in the 1970s, Harrison and his companion William Colvig created a number of American gamelan and authentic Javanese gamelan tuned in Just Intonation, built primarily of aluminum bars and plates. As two of the best known advocates of Just Intonation in the twentieth century, Partch and Harrison have inspired a number of younger composers interested in Just Intonation, including Dean Drummond, Cris Forster, Kraig Grady, David Rosenthal, Daniel Schmidt, and the author to build and compose for ensembles in which idiophones play a prominent role.

Aside from the beauty and variety of their timbres and their association with well known Just Intonation composers, there are two other significant factors that help to account for the popularity of idiophones. The first is ease of construction. Just about anyone can muster the skills, tools, and materials necessary to build a metallophone from aluminum bars or steel conduit tubing. The result may or may not be visually impressive, depending on the quality of one's carpentry, but will probably be quite satisfactory aurally. The second factor is that the tuning is built into the instrument, and remains reasonably stable over long periods of playing. Hence, the intonation of these instruments is not at all affected by the skills (or lack thereof) of the players (as would be the case with wind or unfretted stringed instruments); neither do they require frequent retunings, as would a harp, psaltery, harpsichord, or other multi-stringed instrument. Both of these factors contribute to the appeal of idiophones to intonational explorers. On the negative side, idiophones, once built, are totally inflexible intonationally. This factor is likely to discourage the exploration of a wide variety of tunings.

Having composed primarily for American gamelan for several years, and having since gone on to work with MIDI systems, using primarily harmonic timbres, I think I am in a good position to evaluate the relative merits of inharmonic and harmonic timbres for Just Intonation. My conclusions are as follows: The use of idiophones to perform music in Just Intonation is certainly aesthetically valid. My own initial determination to work with Just Intonation resulted directly from playing in Lou Harrison's first American gamelan in 1975, and recent performances by this ensemble in conjunction with Harrison's seventy-fifth birthday have reminded me of its great beauty. However, there is also no escaping the conclusion that idiophones (or other sound sources lacking harmonic partials) define intervals less precisely than do instruments that produce sustainable tones with harmonic partials. This is especially the case for instruments with wooden sounding bodies, which produce tones of quite short duration. For this reason, I think it is a mistake to limit one's experience with Just Intonation exclusively or primarily to idiophones. The experience of hearing and tuning just intervals on instruments with harmonic partials is an important step in refining one's skills in interval recognition and discrimination. One who lacks such skills is likely to make false choices, especially in dealing with inharmonic timbres. Also, it is extremely desirable to have the experience of hearing and experimenting with a great variety of tunings prior to committing time and money to building an ensemble of idiophones, which will be permanently fixed in a particular tuning.

The ear (my ear, at least) more readily accepts intervals with relatively complex ratios when they are presented in timbres with widely spaced, inharmonic partials than when they are presented in timbres with a full complement of harmonics. Whether this is a virtue or not is debatable. On the one hand, this property makes it easier to introduce intervals based on higher primes or subharmonic-series-based chords, without introducing an unacceptable degree of roughness (this may account, in part, for Partch's combined preference for the eleven limit, subharmonic materials, and idiophones). On the other hand, this same property makes idiophones equally forgiving of irrational intervals. My own aesthetic preference at present is to use no interval or chord with idiophones that would not sound acceptable on instruments with harmonic partials.

The best way to tune idiophones in Just Intonation, in my opinion, is to tune the fundamentals to simple ratios and to ignore the partials entirely. Some composers, most notably Wendy Carlos, have suggested that, for bodies with inharmonic partials, it is more suitable to base tunings on the matching of inharmonic partials than on simple ratios between fundamentals.[11] This may be an appropriate approach for an instrument such as the piano (see above), where partials deviate from the harmonic series in a consistent and predicable manner, but there are several reasons why this approach seems inappropriate for idiophones.

1. In an ensemble with many different varieties of idiophones, such as the Partch ensemble or a gamelan, there are a great many different types of sounding bodies, with different collections of inharmonic partials. A tuning that matched the partials of one instrument or family of instruments would be almost certain to mismatch those of another. The same problem would result in an ensemble that combined harmonic and inharmonic timbres.

2. Even among the sounding bodies on a single instrument, there are significant variations in the relative frequencies of the partials, resulting from the cuttings, hammerings, grindings, or other operations used to tune the bodies. Hence, it is not really possible to create a tuning that matches the partials precisely within a single instrument, unless the partials themselves are systematically retuned.

3. The intervals that would result from matching the inharmonic partials of idiophones would be unlikely to produce good matches with the "neurological template" that creates the sensation of periodicity pitch, and hence would be less likely to function as perceptual gestalts.

Tuning the fundamentals of idiophones accurately requires some kind of electronic tuning device, such as strobe tuner, frequency counter, or oscilloscope. An adjustable lowpass or bandpass filter is also useful for separating the fundamental from the partials. It is not possible to tune the sounding bodies of an idiophone to one another by ear, because of their lack of harmonics, and it is very difficult to tune an idiophone to an accurate unison with a tone with harmonic partials, such as that of a monochord string. Tuning a unison to an electronically generated pure tone is somewhat easier, but once the two tones come within the limit of frequency discrimination it is impossible to tell whether the pitch of the idiophone is above or below the reference except by trial and error. An electronic device that provides visual feedback will give far quicker and more accurate results, and is well worth the expense.

The actual method for tuning an idiophone involves cutting, grinding, or filing to remove material from selected locations to either raise or lower pitch. In the case of a rectangular bar, the bar is shortened (material removed from one or both ends) to raise pitch, and material is removed from the middle (usually on the underside) to lower pitch. Unlike strings, the frequencies of rectangular bars are *not* in simple inverse proportion to their lengths, although frequency does go up as length is decreased. The frequency of a rectangular bar also increases with increasing thickness, the opposite of what happens with strings. Calculating the dimensions of a vibrating bar or other idiophone needed to produce a particular frequency involves rather advanced math and requires that one know the modulus of elasticity for the material in use. This may be useful for an industrial engineer, but for the average composer/instrument builder, trial and error will work just as well.

WIND INSTRUMENTS

All wind instruments depend to a large degree upon the breath support and embouchure of the player for the control of intonation, and are, therefore, at least somewhat amenable to coaxing into Just Intonation. It seems reasonable to expect that a skilled player on almost any woodwind or brass instrument could correctly produce five-limit diatonic or chromatic Just Intonation without too much difficulty, given an example to emulate. Tuning schemes that deviate more radically from equal temperament are more problematic, but skilled players who are willing to commit sufficient rehearsal time can accomplish much. An extensive though not exhaustive collection of alternative fingerings for various wind instruments and equally various microtonal tuning systems was published in Volume 1, Number 4 of *Pitch*.[12] Instruments represented include flute, recorder, oboe, bassoon, clarinet, french horn, and saxophone. Also included is a "fingerography" of other published microtonal fingering charts. Some of the fingerings are for explicitly just systems, while others are for microtonal temperaments such as twenty-four, thirty-one, and seventy-two equal, but all are likely to prove useful in finding the nearest approach to a given just tone on a particular instrument. The authors of these various fingering charts all had much the same things to say about the subjects of microtonality and alternative fingerings:

1. You can't just "push and blow" and expect to get accurate intonation. You must use your ears, breath, and embouchure in coordination (this is, of course, just as true of equal temperament and standard fingerings).

2. Fingerings that work satisfactorily on one make and model of instrument may not do so on another. Hence, fingering charts should be used only as guidelines and each player must discover what works best on his or her instrument.

3. Alternate fingerings on wind instruments will produce variations in timbre and volume as well as pitch. The resulting tones may or may not be acceptable in a given musical context.

The most obvious conclusion to be drawn from the above is that a great many unconventional pitches can be produced on conventional wind instruments, provided that the players are willing to invest sufficient effort. It also suggests that the composer would be well advised to be on hand with a pencil to make adjustments if some of the required tones prove impossible to produce or unacceptable in timbre. It would be a good idea to write some short studies in your desired tuning and get them tried out by sympathetic players before beginning your magnum opus.

The situation for brass players is much the same as for woodwinds, except that the player's lip and ear take on even greater importance, because the lips form a more massive vibrating system than do the reeds of woodwind instruments, and hence exercise greater control over pitch. On a typical three-valved brass instrument, there will be many different valve and harmonic combinations that produce what is ostensibly "the same pitch," but which, in fact, produce different microtonal inflections, offering a variety of choices for the closest approach to the nearest just pitch. Of course, it is well to remember that brass instruments by nature play a harmonic series, and that a valved brass instrument is really just several natural horns conveniently packaged for one player. By making proper adjustments of the tuning slides and by carefully selecting scales that make maximum use of natural harmonics, a great deal of Just Intonation can be gotten out of any brass instrument. Hornist Bruce Heim states that most horn players should be able to produce, at minimum, accurate deviations of 16 cents, and that the –31 cent shift necessary to produce harmonic sevenths is within the reach of many players. Heim has designed a series of exercises to help brass players achieve facility in such intonational shifts.[13]

CONTINUOUS-PITCH INSTRUMENTS

In at least one sense, the instruments best suited for Just Intonation are those which have no pitch restrictions built in. The most obvious instances are the unfretted strings, the trombone, and the human voice. In these cases, it is not the design or tuning of the instrument but the skills of the players or singers that determine the results. Of course, this can be something of a mixed blessing. On a fixed-pitch instrument, once properly tuned, good and poor players alike will produce the limited number of tones available with the proper intonation. On a continuous-pitch instrument, a player with a good ear and the proper training might produce a great number of pitches with the desired accuracy, whereas a poor player might fail to produce even one.

"NATURAL TENDENCIES"

Many writers on intonation have claimed that good singers and string players automatically produce Just Intonation given properly written music and a lack of interference from pianos and other tempered instruments. Conversely, it is also frequently claimed that string players have a "natural tendency" to play in Pythagorean (three-limit) intonation. Quite aside from any such "natural tendency," it appears that many string teachers actively encourage a Pythagorean approach under the name of "expressive intonation." This expressive intonation typically involves the raising of leading tones and a general raising of sharps and lowering of flats relative to equal temperament. Such an approach is the opposite of what is required for harmonic music in five-limit Just Intonation, where sharps are lower than "enharmonically equivalent" flats by the great or enharmonic diesis, and the leading tone, being the 5 identity of the dominant triad, should be played 12 cents flatter than in equal temperament. Given these contradictory claims, it would be best not to rely on the "natural tendencies" of any group of musicians to produce the intonation that you desire, but rather to indicate clearly what intonation your music requires and how it can be reliably achieved. (More will be said about this topic under the heading "Some Thoughts on Obtaining Satisfactory Performances," below.)

BOWED STRINGS

In addition to the difficulties that might result from the intonational training or tendencies of their players, the bowed strings present two other problems where the quest for Just Intonation is concerned. One is vibrato. String players, unless instructed otherwise, play with a more-or-less perpetual vibrato (pitch modulation), which is varied both in depth and speed for expressive purposes. Obviously, such a practice interferes with the precise tuning of consonant intervals, particularly unfamiliar ones. Although the use of vibrato (or any other expressive device) is not precluded in compositions in Just Intonation, it is probably best to regard it as an ornament and use it sparingly, as was the practice in earlier centuries. The second problem concerns the bowing mechanism and its effect on string vibrations. Many observers have reported that bowed strings do not produce clearly defined interference beats in the regions surrounding simple-ratio special relationships, as would, for example, reed instruments or human voices.[14] Recent studies have shown that this is because bowed strings, even in the absence of deliberate vibrato, do not produce vibrations of stable frequency, but rather fluctuate rapidly and randomly over a range as wide as 20 cents. What is perceived as the pitch of a bowed string is actually an average of these random fluctuations. These variations in pitch play a large role in the perceived "warmth" or "richness" of bowed string tone, but also make it difficult for string players to arrive at precise intervals by eliminating beats. Exceptional players, however, may learn to produce sufficiently focused tone to be able to tune by eliminating beats.

Given the difficulties cited above in tuning precise intervals by ear, it seems obvious that markings on the fingerboard could aid string players in playing unfamiliar tunings. However, as Harry Partch expressed the matter, most string players would rather be caught in an unnatural act than be seen with markings on their fingerboards. Whether most contemporary string players are more receptive to such devices than those Partch encountered, I would not care to speculate. In any event, if you should attempt to mark a fingerboard to indicate just intervals, keep the following facts in mind: the oft stated law that the frequency of a string is inversely proportional to its length applies only to an ideal string having uniform density, no thickness and unlimited elasticity. Real strings approach this condition, but do not approach it so closely that such measurements can be relied upon to locate precise tones on a fingerboard. The matter is further complicated because when a string is pressed against a fingerboard, the string is lengthened and its tension is increased, both of which factors affect its pitch. Thus, it will not do to simply measure the length of a string from nut to bridge and mark divisions corresponding to simple fractions of the string length, such as one-half for the octave, two-thirds for the perfect fifth, and so on. Such calculations will produce tones that are noticeably sharp. The best procedure is to check positions against some reliable standard such as a monochord, programmable synthesizer, or electronic tuner. Note, however, that bow pressure is also a factor in string intonation, so fingerboard markings alone cannot be relied upon to produce accurate intonation. I have found that graphic arts tapes, which are available in a great variety of widths and colors, make excellent and harmless temporary fingerboard markers. If you wish to have your works performed properly by string ensembles that are not under your immediate supervision, the preparation of a tuning tape seems advisable (more on this topic below). String quartets in Just Intonation written by Ben Johnston and Terry Riley have received satisfactory performances, but from exceptional rather than average players. I do not know what techniques were used to teach the players the proper intonation in these cases. Lou Harrison has composed several works for small string ensembles in combination with other instruments, but in these cases fixed-pitch instruments such as retuned pianos or harps have been used to anchor the intonation.

VOICES

Where vocalists are concerned, training is everything. Unfortunately, most Western singers have been taught to sing with the accompaniment of the tempered piano, which can never result in precise and stable intonation. The human voice produces tones with pure harmonic partials, and hence singers can tune precise simple-ratio intervals by eliminating beats. Probably the best way to cultivate this capability is to sing against a drone of controlled pitch with a harmonic-rich timbre. The Indian *tamboura* or *sruti* box, which were designed for this precise purpose, make good choices, if available.[15] Otherwise, any instrument that produces a stable, sustained tone with a full complement of harmonic partials will be satisfactory. An appropriate voicing on a synthesizer or electronic organ can work well for this purpose. Because of its inharmonicity, a piano, even if justly tuned, makes a poor accompaniment for vocal practice. Once you have attained facility in tuning just intervals, the practice of properly conceived harmonic music in duos, trios, or quartets with one voice per part is also highly recommended.[16] As is the case with string players, if you are accustomed to sing with perpetual vibrato, it would be well to lose it, at least temporarily, and after having mastered precise intonation, to use it only sparingly.

TROMBONES

The trombone, and its Renaissance ancestor, the sackbut, are potentially among the finest instruments for Just Intonation, although their capabilities have not as yet been fully exploited. They have the same flexibility of pitch as the bowed strings, but produce a timbre with stable harmonic partials, and hence have the ability to precisely tune simple-ratio intervals through the elimination of beats. The trombone has been used by Lou Harrison in a variety of ensemble pieces, including *The Tomb of Charles Ives*, *Four Strict Songs for Eight Baritones and Orchestra*, and the *Concerto for Piano and Selected Orchestra*. Rob Bethea, the lead trombonist with La Monte Young's Theatre of Eternal Music, has been rehearsing Young's *The Second Dream of the High-Tension Line Stepdown Transformer* from *The Four Dreams of China* since 1992.

MIDI SYNTHESIZERS

There are a number of different approaches to the production of Just Intonation on MIDI-equipped instruments. The two principal methods involve pitch bend and user-programmable tuning tables. There is also a technique that combines these two approaches.

PITCH BEND

Pitch bend is a MIDI channel message, that is, it affects all of the notes that are sounded by devices that are set to receive and respond to messages sent over a given MIDI channel. Pitch bend is defined in the MIDI specification as a 14-bit controller; that is, it divides the pitch-bend range, which is normally set at the receiving instrument, into 2^{14} or 16,384 parts. Unlike most MIDI controllers, pitch bend is bipolar; the available resolution is split into two parts, representing positive and negative bend (raising or lowering pitch), with a central value of zero, representing no pitch bend. Hence, the 16,384 step range should be viewed as ±8,192. If the range were set to semitone, normally the narrowest range available, this would result in a pitch resolution of 0.012 cents, fine enough to satisfy even the most demanding ears. Regrettably, this high degree of precision is seldom, if ever, achieved in practice. The MIDI specification requires that MIDI instruments send and receive pitch-bend messages with 14-bit resolution, but it does not require that they respond to all 14 bits of the message, and in fact, few current instruments do so. Typically, MIDI instruments discard the 7 least-significant bits of the pitch-bend message, leaving a resolution of 7 bits; 128 or ±64 steps. With a pitch-bend range of a semitone, this yields a much cruder pitch resolution of 1.56 cents, resulting in a maximum error of 0.78 cents—not egregious when compared to the errors of equal temperament, but certainly detectable when simple intervals are sounded with sustained tones having harmonic partials.

Pitch bend as a tuning method is generally applied in conjunction with MIDI mode 4 (Omni-off/Poly), in which the different "voices" of a polytimbral instrument respond to different MIDI channels. Because the MIDI specification only recognizes sixteen channels, a maximum of sixteen different notes with *different* pitch-bend amounts can be sounded at one time. This limit can be overcome by the use of a multiport MIDI system, which can have up to sixteen channels on each port. Although one could conceivably manually edit sequencer files and add the appropriate amount of pitch bend for each and every tone, this would be extremely tedious. A more practical approach involves the use of a computer program to "post-process" files created by a conventional sequencer. Composer Jules Siegel has developed such a system, which he uses in conjunction with the "Personal Composer" program.[17] A detailed description of this system is beyond the scope of this publication, but the basic premise is comparatively simple. A table is constructed containing the amounts by which various tones of the tempered scale must be bent in order to match selected just "equivalents" for a given key. The program then examines a sequencer file in combination with a silent "reference track" (a sort of inaudible cantus firmus that indicates which keynote and reference tone other notes in the sequence should be tuned in reference to) and uses the table to calculate the amount of pitch bend that needs to be applied to each note. "Patches" can be inserted in the reference track to override the values in the table under special circumstances. Siegel has used this method in many compositions with apparent success. He has not, however, made his software available to the public, so anyone wishing to attempt this method will have to write their own, a task that will require at least an intermediate knowledge of computer programming and MIDI.

A similar approach can be used to produce just tunings via pitch bend in live performance. Data from a keyboard or other MIDI controller is routed to a computer, which uses a table to determine appropriate intonation for different pitches and routes them to the appropriate MIDI channels along with the necessary pitch-bend messages. Present day processors are fast enough that a program of this type, if properly written, could operate on a complex data stream without introducing audible delay. And, of course, such a system would not need to be limited to twelve tones per octave, or any other fixed limit, since the program, in addition to mapping appropriate channel assignments and bend amounts, could remap key events to other notes. To make a system such as this really flexible would require some additional input that would indicate the current key or tuning reference, analogous to Siegel's "reference track," but operating in real time. The ideal solution, short of a direct mind interface, would be to use a pedal board, as this would leave both hands free for playing. Barring this, a certain range of the keyboard might be reserved for tuning selection, or the computer keyboard could be used.

Instruments with User-Programmable Tuning Tables

Since the late 1970s, a number of synthesizers and samplers have offered explicit support for alternate tunings by means of preset or programmable tuning tables. (We won't examine the features of specific instruments here, as the market life of a given make and model tends to be short, and new models with different features are always appearing.) The tuning of any digitally controlled instrument is represented by a series of numbers which are typically stored in ROM as a part of the instrument's operating software. When a key is pressed, the software looks up the number, combines it with values representing pitch bend and pitch modulation (vibrato), and routes it to the pitch control circuitry, which responds by producing the appropriate frequency. On an instrument which supports only equal temperament, only one such table is provided, and modification by the user is not possible. On an instrument that supports alternate tunings, additional tables are available, either other preset tunings representing historical or world music scales, or user programmable tunings stored in RAM. The most practical instruments for serious composition in Just Intonation are those which include storage space for a significant number of user-programmed tunings and allow tuning tables to be selected under MIDI program control, a feature which, unfortunately, is still uncommon. Preset tunings, though not without value, particularly for the comparison of historical tunings, are too limited and inflexible to be of much use for just compositions, although their usefulness can be increased by a method described below.

There are a number of ways that an instrument with programmable tuning tables can be used. Which is most suitable depends on whether you are recording or performing live, and on the precise capabilities of the instrument(s) you are using. I normally work in a MIDI recording studio, using Yamaha DX/TX series instruments. My normal practice is to program a number of twelve-tone, octave-repeating scales covering the gamut I expect to use in a composition, usually with considerable overlap between the different tunings. I use a commercial sequencer program and embed system-exclusive messages in the sequences to switch tuning tables as the composition requires. The instruments that I use can store up to sixty-five programmed tunings, so I have never experienced a practical limitation as to the number of pitches available for a particular composition. My method would not be nearly as suitable, however, for live performance.

Practical Just Intonation with Real Instruments

If one wished to perform a composition in real time that involved more than twelve tones per octave, a better approach might be to program a tuning that placed all of the required tones on the keyboard at one time.[18] This approach, of course, has problems of its own, the most obvious being the more difficult fingerings that would result from having an octave occupy more physical space on the keyboard. Another potential problem is that a typical MIDI synthesizer has a keyboard that covers only five octaves. Hence, if one were to program a tuning of twenty-four tones per octave, for example, only two and one-half octaves would be available at one time on a conventional keyboard. This problem can be mitigated somewhat, albeit at increased expense, by using a MIDI master keyboard controller, which typically has a range of eight octaves. However, even this approach does not allow instant access to all 128 different pitches (10.67 octaves) that are potentially available on a MIDI instrument. The use of two five-octave keyboards might be the best approach here.

Even in live performance, it may be possible to use the tuning-table-switching technique. If one plays in conjunction with a sequenced accompaniment, commands embedded in the sequences can control the tuning table selection for both live and sequenced parts. Even if one doesn't use sequences in performance, it is possible to use a sequencer to play a silent tuning-control track, although in this case it would be necessary to listen to some kind of cue track to maintain synchronization with the sequencer. Another possibility is to use some kind of separate MIDI controller, perhaps using pedals or foot switches, to send preprogrammed commands to change tuning tables. Or an offstage technician could send the commands as required. A great many other possibilities will probably suggest themselves to experienced MIDI musicians.

TUNING TABLES PLUS PITCH BEND

Some instruments have preset tuning tables, including some forms of Just Intonation, that can be transposed to different "keynotes."[19] Unfortunately, although this feature allows music to be performed in a fixed scale in a variety of keys, it is not as useful for modulation or transposition in Just Intonation as one might expect. The problem is that these instruments lack the intelligence to take into account the relations between keys and select a precise transposition that maintains the proper common-tone relationships. Instead, the transpositions are to a fixed gamut of twelve keynotes, which may correspond to the twelve tones of equal temperament, or to some other arbitrary standard. This problem can be cured by the use of pitch bend. For example, if you intend to modulate from C major to E major, and you want the relation between C and E to be 5:4 (386 cents), but the transposition factor your instrument uses is a tempered major third (400 cents), simply add the amount of negative pitch bend equivalent to 14 cents, or the closest approximation thereto that your instrument is capable of. Keep in mind that you have to know the real pitch bend resolution of your instrument to determine this. Pitch bend can be conveniently used this way because once a pitch bend command has been sent on a given MIDI channel, the channel remains "bent" and all subsequent notes played on that channel are affected until a new pitch bend message is received. Hence, it is only necessary to send a single pitch bend message per channel, per transposition.

THE MIDI TUNING-DUMP SPECIFICATION

In January 1992, the MIDI Manufacturers Association and its Japanese equivalent, the JMA, adopted an extension to the MIDI specification concerned with alternate tunings. (For a copy of the specification, contact the International MIDI Association, 5316 W. 57th Street, Los Angeles, CA 90056; (310) 649-6434.) This MIDI Tuning Specification was initially proposed by a committee of Just Intonation Network members organized by composer Robert Rich in 1988. Many features of the tuning specification had their origins in a "wish list" compiled by the author. The formal specification was written by Carter Scholz, and lobbying for the spec before industry organizations was done primarily by Rich. The specification is concerned primarily with permitting the transfer of tuning data among instruments from different manufacturers, a feat which was heretofore impossible without the use of translation software.

The MIDI Tuning Specification uses a 21-bit data word to specify frequency. The first byte indicates the nearest tempered semitone, specified in terms of the standard MIDI note range of 0–127, and the remaining two bytes specify a fraction of a semitone *above* the indicated note. This 14 bits-per-semitone specification translates to a pitch resolution of 0.0061 cents, twice as precise as the finest resolution theoretically available via pitch bend. Unfortunately, as with pitch bend, and most other aspects of the MIDI specification, the tuning spec simply indicates the format in which data describing tunings will be transmitted and received. It does not require that any MIDI instrument support alternate tunings in any form, much less that they provide the high degree of frequency resolution that the data format is capable of representing. Indeed, the specification says explicitly that "any instrument that does not support the full suggested resolution may discard any unneeded lower bits on reception." The fourteen bits-per-semitone resolution in the specification is intended to "be stringent enough to satisfy most demands of music and experimentation." It is not likely that any commercial manufacturers of musical instruments will begin to use the kind of hardware necessary to meet the specified resolution in the near future.

In addition to the format for tuning data exchange, the MIDI Tuning Specification also defines messages for changing the active tuning table and for changing the tuning of a single note "on the fly." An important aspect of the specification is that it requires that both of these messages "take effect immediately, and must occur without audible artifacts (note-off, resets, retriggers, glitches, etc.) if any affected notes are sounding when the message is received." This description is contrary to and a direct consequence of the behavior of some instruments that were on the market at the time the specification was originally conceived. For example, on the Yamaha DX7 II/TX802, a change in tuning does not affect any note that is currently sounding when the tuning change message is received; a sounding note must be released and restruck in order for a tuning change to take effect.

At the time of this writing, it is difficult to say what effect, if any, the MIDI Tuning Specification will have on the development of future MIDI instruments. At the very least, it will make all manufacturers aware that the possibility of supporting alternate tunings exists, and give those who choose to implement such a feature some guidelines to follow. Beyond this, we can but hope.

SOME THOUGHTS ON
OBTAINING SATISFACTORY PERFORMANCES

If you write a score for conventional instruments, peppered with ratios, cents deviations, or exotic accidentals such as are used in this publication, and send it out to make its way in the world, your efforts will be unlikely to meet with much success. The obvious reason for this is that few musicians have been trained either to understand and interpret such symbols or to produce the intervals that they represent. The best solution is to be actively involved in the rehearsal and performance of one's own music, or barring this, to seek performances only from the relative handful of musicians who have established reputations for performing music in Just Intonation. Where this is not possible, however, there are some things that can be done to make a satisfactory performance more likely. The first of these concerns not scoring but composition. Know whether what your scores demand is possible with the instruments you specify and with players of average ability. If your music requires intonational virtuosity of the highest order, then so be it, but don't waste your time submitting such pieces to musicians who lack the necessary skills or the commitment to develop them. In compositions intended for players inexperienced with Just Intonation, consider the inclusion of at least one fixed-pitch instrument (retuned piano or harpsichord, harp, electronic keyboard, guitar) to help "anchor" the intonation and perhaps play a sort of continuo role, if that is compatible with your aesthetic goals. If you don't play the instruments that your compositions require, try to consult with experienced, sympathetic players before or during the compositional process, if such people can be found. On the other hand, don't be discouraged if conventionally trained players tell you that what you are trying to do is useless or crazy.

Having produced a score and decided who might have the necessary skills to perform it, give the musicians as much help as possible in understanding your intentions. In particular, it can be extremely valuable to mark up your score to indicate which pitches are consonant with which others, which are dissonances, who should listen to whom for the tuning of particular intervals, and the like. You may think that all these relationships are obvious from a statement of your tuning at the head of your score, and it might be so to someone who was fluent in the language of Just Intonation, but give your players all the help you can in understanding this unfamiliar language. Always keep in mind that you are requiring people to do something that they have not been trained or accustomed to do.

If your score requires the retuning of a piano or other fixed-pitch instrument, be sure to include *detailed* instructions as to which primary intervals are to be tuned and in what order, what secondary intervals and what chords should be used as checks, and so on. Cents deviations from equal temperament may come in handy if an electronic tuner is to be used, but remember that such indications can serve only as guideposts, as a tuning that works satisfactorily on one piano or harpsichord will not necessarily "transplant" successfully to another, due to differing degrees of inharmonicity. This is especially true for instruments of different sizes. Be sure to indicate this in your tuning instructions.

The other thing you can do is to make tuning/rehearsal tapes or CDs of your pieces. In teaching musicians to play unfamiliar intervals, no amount of verbal description can substitute for actually hearing the intervals. Such tapes can be as simple as statements of scales and important chords, or can include full versions of individual parts, "music-minus-one" arrangements, or even complete performances of compositions with full instrumentation. Computers and synthesizers are extremely useful for the production of such tapes, even for composers who intend for their compositions to be performed exclusively on acoustic instruments. And the value to the composer of the ability to hear his or her compositions and to be sure that the specified intonation works as intended *before* submitting them for performance cannot be ignored.

NOTES

Chapter 1 Notes:

1. Partch, Harry. *Genesis of a Music,* 2d ed. New York: Da Capo Press, 1974

2. Barbour, J. Murray. *Tuning and Temperament.* New York: Da Capo Press, 1972.

3. From ancient times until the seventeenth century, musical intervals were represented as ratios of string lengths, rather than as ratios of frequencies. Since for a string of a given density, stretched at a given tension, frequency of vibration is inversely proportional to string length, it is only necessary to invert string-length ratios to transform them to frequency ratios.

4. The use of the term "Just Intonation" in English is of comparatively recent origin. The earliest citation in the *Oxford English Dictionary*, General Perronet Thompson's *On the Principles and Practice of Just Intonation*, dates from 1850.

5. I refer here to the viol family used in the Renaissance and early baroque, which consisted of instruments with six strings, equipped with frets, rather than to the modern violin family, which uses four strings and no frets.

6. Meantone, unlike equal temperament, is an "open" system. That is, its flatted fifths do not form a closed circle. Hence, it is possible to get more good triads and keys in meantone by tuning more than twelve tones per octave, as was sometimes done. Meantone fifths very nearly form a closed circle after 31 fifths, and if so extended, meantone is virtually indistinguishable from 31-tone equal temperament. The "good" triads in meantone are not just triads, having a just major third and a slightly flattened minor third and perfect fifth. They are "good" only in the relative context of the meantone system.

7. The earliest mathematically correct exposition of twelve-tone equal temperament comes not from Europe but from China, where prince Zhu Zai-yu published the correct formula in 1596. The Chinese, however, did not make any practical use of this discovery, considering it a mere mathematical curiosity, and there is no evidence that the Chinese discovery influenced the development of temperament in the West.

8. Harrison, Lou. "Four Strict Songs for Eight Baritones and Orchestra." Louisville Orchestra First Edition Records, LOU-58-2 (out of print); A revised version for full chorus (1992) is on *Lou Harrison: A Birthday Celebration.* Musical Heritage Society CD 513616L.

Chapter 2 Notes:

1. Pitch *discrimination* is poor for tones with frequencies above about 4kHz and, in fact, tones with such high frequencies are rarely employed in music. However, high frequency components contribute to the timbres of complex tones with lower frequencies.

2. Actually, timbre involves other factors than the steady-state waveform of a sound. The way in which the waveform changes over time, especially during the onset or attack portion of a tone, has been shown to play an extremely important role in establishing the characteristic sounds of various instruments. The presence of fixed resonance bands or formants in various instruments is also a significant aspect of timbre. While these phenomena are worthy of every musician's attention, they are outside the scope of this study.

3. Harmonic (or nearly harmonic) components are characteristic of tones produced by vibrating strings and by cylindrical or conical air columns. Other sounding bodies, such as bars, plates, and stretched membranes, produce sets of components with much more complex relationships.

4. The law in question, which applies to all periodic vibrations, not merely to sound, is known as Fourier's theorem, after its discoverer, the French mathematician, Jean Baptiste Fourier (1768–1830). The process of deconstructing a complex wave into its simple components is known as Fourier analysis; conversely, the process of adding simple components to construct a desired complex wave is known as Fourier synthesis.

5. One can learn, under certain circumstances, to distinguish some of the lower harmonics making up a complex musical tone, but our normal mode of hearing is *synthetic* rather than *analytic*. Were it not for this fact, music as we know it could not exist.

6. Noise, however, sometimes plays a significant role in music.

7. This is true in theory, but in practice the strength of the harmonics of musical tones typically diminishes rapidly in higher octaves. Hence, in intervals wider than two octaves (4:1), there may be little interaction between the harmonics of the higher tone and the relatively high harmonics of the lower tone.

8. The difference in Hz between the successive harmonics of a complex tone is equal to the frequency of the fundamental. For instance, for a tone of 100Hz, the second harmonic has a frequency of 200Hz, the third has a frequency of 300Hz, the fourth has a frequency of 400Hz, and so forth. Thus, the difference between any two consecutive harmonics is 100Hz. Consider the implications for tones in the lowest audible octave (circa 25Hz–50Hz). Such tones have frequencies that fall in the vicinity of the beat frequency which causes the maximum roughness. If such a tone is supplied with harmonic partials, each consecutive pair of partials will beat at a frequency equivalent to the fundamental. Because all of the pairs of partials beat at the same frequency, which is also the perceived frequency of the tone as a whole, the separate beats will not be distinguished, but the tone will have a timbre that is very rough or harsh. Such indeed is perceived to be the case when very low tones are accompanied by many strong harmonics.

9. Benade, Arthur H. *Fundamentals of Musical Acoustics*. New York: Oxford University Press, 1976; reprint, New York: Dover Publications, 1990. pp. 274–275.

Chapter 3 Notes:

1. These conventions are followed in this publication, in **1/1**, and, to a considerable extent, in Harry Partch's *Genesis of a Music*. They are not always followed in other texts dealing with Just Intonation, particularly older publications.

2. In the musical examples in this book, $^1/_1$ will, unless otherwise indicated, be represented by the tone C. This is done strictly for the purpose of making the examples easy to read. In practice, $^1/_1$ can be assigned any frequency whatever. Just Intonation is concerned with pre*cise relative* pitch, that is, with precise interval relations *between* pitches. It is not at all concerned with absolute pitch.

3. A few composers, such as La Monte Young and Glenn Branca, have composed with primes well beyond this limit.

4. Here, 1 is understood as 2^0.

5. Because the ear more easily recognizes the lower identities of the series, fewer low number identities are required to clearly establish a tonality than are higher number identities.

6. Helmholtz, Hermann L. F. *On the Sensations of Tone*, fourth (and last) German edition (1877) translated by Alexander J. Ellis as the second English edition (1885), revised, corrected annotated and with an additional appendix by the translator. New York: Dover Publications (1954), p. 211 (translator's addendum).

7. Chalmers, John H., Jr. *Divisions of the Tetrachord*. Hanover NH.: Frog Peak Music, 1993.

8. This assumes that the three intervals that form the tetrachord are unique. When the tetrachord contains two identical intervals, as, for example, the Pythagorean diatonic tetrachord, which consists of two 9:8s and a 256:243, only three unique permutations are possible.

Chapter 4 Notes:

1. For example, Jean Adam Serre (1704–1788) and Giuseppe Tartini (1692–1770).

2. The fact that it is mathematically impossible for any number of perfect fifths to equal any number of octaves has not stopped many theorists from calculating vast numbers of 3:2s in hopes of finding a match. Some die-hard musical flat-earthers persist in the search even now. Of course, there are points at which chains of 3:2s make close approximations to some number of 2:1s. These "cycles," most notably those of 31 and 53 3:2s, serve as the basis of some of the more popular high-order temperaments.

3. Some theorists would not accept the identification of the open triad as a chord, since it contains only two unique tones, the highest tone being an octave duplicate of the root.

4. Ptolemy and the other Greek harmonists had no knowledge of or interest in triads or in harmony as the term is currently used, and certainly did not construct the syntonon diatonic using the method described above. For Ptolemy, the syntonon diatonic was just one of many diatonic scales with superparticular (x+1:x) ratio intervals between scale degrees.

5. There is a musical structure that forms six just triads (three major and three minor) from seven tones. This is Harry Partch's "incipient tonality diamond" (*Genesis*, p. 110). However, when the tones on the diamond are arranged in order of ascending or descending pitch, they

bear no resemblance to a diatonic scale, or to any familiar scale whatever.

6. Ellis, Alexander J. Translator's additions to Helmholtz's *On the Sensations of Tone,* Section E, pp. 457–464.

7. ibid., p. 462.

17. This is not a chapter note; A^{17} means the pitch A ($^5/_3$) raised by 51:50 (= $^{17}/_{10}$).

Chapter 5 Notes:

1. Hill, Ralph David. "Study in Whole Tones in Two Parts." **1/1**, 5:2 (Spring 1989), pp. 6–7.

2. The best one can do as far as integrating 50:49 into a tetrachord is to divide the just chromatic semitone (25:24) into two parts (50:49 and 49:48). This leaves an undivided interval of 32:25 (427.37 cents), quite a harsh dissonance. It is understandable that the ancients didn't see fit to construct such a scale.

3. Maxwell, Miles. "Heavenly Harmony," part three of the series "Just Intonation Reconsidered," in *The Composer*, Autumn 1973. Reprinted in **1/1**, 2:3 (Summer 1985), pp. 1, 7–9, 15.

4. It is uncertain whether some of these scales saw actual use or whether they were solely the creations of speculative theorists.

5. Keislar, Douglas. "Six American Composers on Nonstandard Tunings." *Perspectives of New Music*, 29:1 (Winter 1991).

6. Partch called chords of this type, based on harmonic series segments, *otonalities* (o as in over). His system also featured *utonality* hexads (u as in under), based on analogous subharmonic series segments, that is, $^1/_4$:$^1/_5$:$^1/_6$:$^1/_7$:$^1/_9$:$^1/_{11}$.

7. Miller, George A. "The Magical Number Seven, Plus or Minus Two: Some Limits on our Capacity for Processing Information." *Psychology Review*, 63:82–89 (1956).

8. Partch. *Genesis of a Music.* p. 159

9. Johnston, Ben. "Rational Structure in Music" *American Society of University Composers Proceedings* I/II (1976–77) pp. 102–108. Reprinted in **1/1**, 2:3 and 2:4, 1986.

10. Chalmers, John H., and Ervin M. Wilson. "Combination Product Sets and Other Harmonic and Melodic Structures." *Proceedings of the 1981 International Computer Music Conference.* North Texas State University, Denton, TX. pp. 348–362.

11. Grady, Kraig. "Ervin Wilson's Hexany." **1/1** 7:1, pp. 8–11.

12. Chalmers, John H. "Tritriadic Transformations" **1/1**, 3:1, pp. 1, 7–9.

13. Galilei, Vincenzo. *Dialogo della musica antica e moderna.* Florence, 1581.

14. Helmholtz. *On the Sensations of Tone.* Translator's note, p. 346.

15. Widener, Ward M. *A Practical Method for Achieving More Perfect Tuning.* Published by the author, 203 Westbrook Drive, Austin, TX 78746.

Chapter 6 Notes:

1. The author speaks from experience.

2. Harrison, Lou. *Lou Harrison's Music Primer.* New York: C.F. Peters Corp., 1971. p. 42.

3. *Experimental Musical Instruments.* P.O. Box 784, Nicasio, CA 94946. *EMI* has ceased publication, but back issues are still available.

4. After Benade, *Fundamentals of Musical Acoustics*, p. 315.

5. ibid.

6. I am indebted for information on this topic to John Schneider's "A History of the Just Guitar" **1/1** 7:3 (March 1992), pp. 11–15.

7. At the time of this writing, from Mark Rankin, P.O. Box 201, Alderpoint, CA 95511. Note, however, that Mr. Rankin rarely maintains a fixed place of residence for very long. Consult the Just Intonation Network for current information.

8. As of September 2002, Hervé R. Chouard, a luthier based in Germany, was offering Vogt-style guitars: http://www.chouard.de/   herve@chouard.de

9. It is possible to adjust the partials in a rectangular wood or metal bar to make them harmonic. This process is normally followed in the production of commercially made American marimbas and vibraphones. The partials of these instruments are normally tuned to a major triad, which accounts for their rather sweet sound. However, none of the composer/instrument builders working with idiophones in Just Intonation adjust the partials of their instruments in this way.

10. For a detailed account of the construction and tuning methods of Partch's instruments, see chapters twelve and thirteen of *Genesis of a Music.*

11. "Tuning: At the Crossroads" *Computer Music Journal*, 11:1 (Spring, 1987) pp. 29–43.

12. *Pitch: for the International Microtonalist*. Spring 1990. The American Festival of Microtonal Music, 318 E. 70th Street, #5FW, New York, NY 10021.

13. Heim, David Bruce. "Practical Tuning, Temperament, and Conditioning for Hornists and Other Wind Instrumentalists: Understanding and Attaining Intonational Flexibility in Musical Performance." (Unpublished Masters Thesis, University of Tulsa, 1990).

14. Benade, Arthur H. *Fundamentals of Musical Acoustics*, p. 549; Partch, *Genesis of a Music*, p. 153.

15. Indeed, a number of Just Intonation composers, most notably La Monte Young and Terry Riley, have gained considerable benefit from the study of North Indian vocal music, which demands considerable intonational sensitivity.

16. That is, music in which consonance rather than dissonance is the norm, and which is composed with proper attention to the requirements and consequences of comma shifts and the like, and free of equal-temperament style tricks of approaching a tone as though it were one pitch and departing it as though it were another.

17. Siegel, Jules. "Algorithmic Tuning Via MIDI" **1/1**, 3:4 (Autumn, 1987). pp. 4–6.

18. Note, however, that not all instruments with programmable tuning capability permit this. Some are limited strictly to twelve-tone octave repeating tunings, or only allow individual notes to be retuned over a restricted range, such as 100 cents.

19. This is distinct from the normal transpose feature common to most MIDI instruments. This feature simply adds or subtracts a certain constant from incoming note numbers, so that playing a given key produces a tone some number of steps higher or lower on the keyboard. This is equivalent to transposition in equal temperament, but does not work for Just Intonation.

INDEX

A

Added-second chord 57
Aeolian scale 39
Alves, William C. 7
American gamelan 6, 7, 66, 72
Anomalies 33. *See also* great diesis, Pythagorean comma, septimal comma, syntonic comma, etc.
Ars Antiqua period 38
Ayers, Lydia 7

B

Bach, J.S. 4
Barbershop quartet 35
Barbour, J. Murray 2
Baroque era 3, 4
Basilar membrane 14, 18
Bassoon 74
Beating harmonics. *See* Harmonics: beating
Beats. *See* Harmonics: beating; Interference beats
Beat frequency (f_B) 13
  due to the inharmonicity of piano strings 68
Benade, Arthur H.
  experiment to identify "special relationships" 22–24
Bethea, Rob 76
Blues 35, 51
Blue notes 35, 55
Boethius, Anicius Manlius Severinus 2
Bosanquet, R.H.M. 5, 70
Bowed string instruments 75
Branca, Glenn 65
Brass instruments 19, 74
Brown, Colin 5, 70

C

Canright, David 7, 71
Carlos, Wendy 73
Catler, Jon 7
Cents 15
  calculation 26
  defined 4
Chalmers, John H.
  tritriadic scales 64
Cheng 71
Chords 30–32. *See also* Triads, other chord names
  condissonant 31
  consonant 31, 46
  dissonant 31
  eleven- and thirteen-limit 62–64
  five-limit 46–48
    condissonant 47–48
  seven-limit 56–59
    condissonant 58–59
    subharmonic 57–58
Chromatic scale 45. *See also* Harmonic duodene

Chromelodeon 70
Circle of fifths 37
Clarinet 19
Classical era 4
Clavichord 67
Clusters. *See* Tone clusters
Cochlea 14
Cocktail-party effect 16
Colvig, William 6, 72
Combination tones. *See* Difference tones; Summation tones
Comma. *See* Pythagorean comma, septimal comma, syntonic comma
Comma of Didymus. *See* Syntonic comma
Common-practice period 6
Common-practice theory 35, 51
Complex tones 19–20
Continuous-pitch instruments 66, 74–76
Critical band 13, 51

D

Difference tones 16–17, 19
  first-order 16
    of condissonant triads 48
    of just major triad 46
    of just minor triad 46–47
    of major-seventh chord 48
    of minor-seventh chord 48
  higher-order 16–17
    of dominant-ninth chord 56
    of dominant-seventh chord 56
    of subharmonic pentad 58
    of tempered major third 17
Diminished-seventh chord 49–50, 64
Diminished major-seventh chord 65
Ditone diatonic. *See* Pythagorean diatonic scale
Divisions of the Tetrachord (book) 34
Dominant-minor-ninth chord 50, 64
Dominant-ninth chord 31, 55, 56, 58, 62
  subsets of 56–57
Dominant-seventh chord 31, 35, 48–49, 51, 55, 56
  subsets of 56–57
Drummond, Dean 7, 72
Duodenarium 46
Duodene. *See* Harmonic duodene

E

Electronic organ 70
Ellis, Alexander J. 26, 31, 45, 64, 70
Enharmonic equivalents 44
Enharmonic spellings 49
Experimental Musical Instruments (periodical) 67

F

False Consonance 54–55
Fender Rhodes Electric Piano 70
Fixed-Pitch Instruments 67–71
Fixed scales 42, 55
  seven-limit 59

Flute 19, 74
Fokker, Adriaan
  method for representing intervals on the lattice 43
Formants 19
Forster, Cris 7, 72
Frantz, Glenn 7
French horn 74
French impressionists 63
Frequency, absolute 11. *See also* Hertz (Hz)
  calculating 28
  of 1/1 36
Frequency ratios 11, 25–29. *See also* Just Intervals
  calculations with 25–29
    addition 25
    complementation 26
    converting to cents 26
    division 26–28
    subtraction 25–26
  converting to harmonic or subharmonic series segment 28–29
  only unambiguous inerval names 32
  rules and conventions for using 25
  superparticular 27
Fretted instruments 3, 71
Fullman, Ellen 7
Fused tone 13, 14

G

Galilei, Vincenzo
  proposed fretting for the lute 64
Genesis of a Music 2, 6, 67, 70
Grady, Kraig 7, 72
Great diesis 44–45, 50
Guitar 71

H

Hair cells 14
Half-diminished-seventh chord 55, 56–57
Harmonics 15, 16. *See also* Harmonic series; Partials: harmonic
  beating 20–24
    of an octave (2:1) 20–21
    of a perfect fifth (3:2) 21–22
    of a unison (1:1) 20
  coincident (matching) 20–24
  formula for 21
  of just intervals (figure) 21
  of just major triad 46
  of just minor triad 46
Harmonic and subharmonic series (figure) 29
Harmonic duodene 45–46
Harmonic series 4, 14–16, 18, 19, 28–30
  defined 14
  fundamental of 15, 19, 31
  missing. *See* Periodicity pitch
Harmonic spectrum 15, 19
  cutoff frequency of 19
  of strings 19
Harmonists (ancient Greek theorists) 2
Harp 70, 72

Harpsichord 67, 72
Harrison, Lou 6, 66, 72, 75
   Concerto for Piano with Javanese Gamelan 69
   Concerto for Piano with Selected Orchestra 69, 76
   Four Strict Songs for Eight Baritones and Orchestra 6, 76
   The Tomb of Charles Ives 76
Harrison, Michael 7, 69
   From Ancient Worlds 68
Heim, Bruce 74
Helmholtz, Hermann von 4–5, 45, 70
Heptad 62, 63
Hertz (Hz) 10, 11. *See also* Periodic vibration: frequency
Hexad 62, 63
Hill, Ralph David 7, 54
Hohner Clavinet 70
Hykes, David 7

I

Identities
   as defining characteristics of a chord 30, 31
   defined 30
Idiophones 19, 72–73
Industrial revolution 5
Interference Beats 12–13, 46. *See also* Harmonics: beating
Intermodulation products. *See* Difference tones, Summation tones
Interval 10–11. *See also* Frequency ratios; Just intervals
   conventional names for 10, 32
   defined 10
   harmonic vs subharmonic interpretation 28
Intonation Systems 71

J

Jazz 35, 51
Johnston, Ben 6, 75
   notation for Just Intonation 33
   ratio scales 64
   remarks on 11 and 13 61
   Sonata for Microtonal Piano 70
Just Intervals
   1:1 (unison) 36
   2:1 (octave) 36, 37, 44
   3:1 (perfect twelfth) 24
   3:2 (perfect fifth) 36, 37, 38, 39, 40, 42, 45, 46, 51, 54, 55, 57, 59
   4:1 (double octave) 24
   4:3 (perfect fourth) 33, 36, 37, 38, 40, 42, 54, 55
   5:1 24
   5:2 (major tenth) 24
   5:3 (major sixth) 24, 39
   5:4 (major third) 38, 39, 40, 42, 45, 46, 50, 51, 55, 56, 57, 58
   6:1 24
   6:5 (minor third) 24, 39, 45, 49, 50
   7:1 24
   7:2 24, 51
   7:3 (septimal minor or subminor tenth) 24, 51
   7:4 (harmonic, subminor, or septimal minor seventh) 35, 51
   7:5 (most consonant tritone) 23, 51, 55, 57
   7:6 (subminor or septimal minor third) 23, 51, 55, 57, 58, 59
   8:1 (triple octave) 24
   8:3 24
   8:5 (minor sixth) 24, 39, 40, 41, 42, 50, 55
   8:7 (septimal whole tone; supermajor second) 23, 24, 51, 54, 55, 57
   9:4 (major ninth) 24, 37
   9:5 (acute minor seventh) 40, 49, 56, 57
   9:7 (supermajor third) 55, 56, 57, 58, 59
   9:8 (major whole tone) 33, 37, 38, 40, 55, 64, 65
   10:3 24
   10:7 (septimal tritone) 51, 55
   10:9 (minor whole tone) 40, 55
   11:1, 11:2, 11:3, 11:4, 11:5 24
   11:6 62
   11:8 (primary interval for 11) 61, 62
   11:9 (neutral third) 62
   11:10 62
   12:5 (minor tenth) 24
   12:7 51
   12:11 62
   13:1, 13:2, 13:3, 13:4, 13:5, 13:6 24
   13:8 (primary interval for 13) 61, 62
   13:9 62
   13:10 62
   15:8 (diatonic major seventh) 40
   15:13 62
   15:14 54, 55
   16:5 24
   16:9 (minor seventh) 37, 49
   16:11 62
   16:13 62
   16:15 (diatonic semitone) 40, 45, 55
   17:16 64
   17:16 (primary interval for 17) 64
   18:11 62
   18:17 64
   19:16 (primary interval for 19) 64
   21:16 (septimal subfourth) 54, 55
   21:20 54, 55
   25:16 50
   25:24 (small chromatic semitone) 45, 55
   27:16 (Pythagorean major sixth) 37
   27:20 (acute, imperfect, or wolf fourth) 40
   27:25 (great limma) 45
   28:25 (intermediate septimal whole tone) 54
   28:27 54, 55
   32:21 54, 55
   32:25 (diminished fourth) 45, 50
   32:27 (Pythagorean minor third) 37, 41, 49
   33:32 62
   35:32 (small septimal whole tone) 54
   36:25 (acute diminished fifth) 49
   36:35 (septimal quarter tone or diesis) 54
   40:27 (grave, imperfect, or "wolf" fifth) 40, 41
   49:48 (septimal sixth tone) 54
   50:49 (septimal sixth tone) 54
   64:63. *See* Septimal comma (64:63)
   65:64 62
   75:64 (augmented second) 45
   81:64 (Pythagorean major third, ditone) 36, 37, 38, 40, 41
   81:80. *See* Syntonic comma
   128:81 (Pythagorean minor sixth) 37, 40
   128:125. *See* Great diesis
   135:128 (large limma, large chromatic semitone) 45
   243:128 (Pythagorean major seventh) 40
   256:243 (Pythagorean limma) 37, 40
Just Intonation
   defined 1–2
   discovery 2
   eleven- and thirteen-limit 59–63
   five-limit 35, 38–50, 75
      difficiencies of 48–50
   obtaining satisfactory performances in 79–80
   seven-limit 51–59
      coloristic use of 55
   seventeen- and nineteen-limit 64–65
   three-limit 36–38
   twentieth-century revival 6–7
Just Intonation Network 8, 78

K

Keyboard instruments 3, 4, 67–70
   Acoustic 67–70
   electroacoustic 70
Koto 71

L

Lattice
   complementation on 44
   five-limit 42–44
      figure 43
   seven-limit 51
      figure 52, 53
   syntonon diatonic (figure) 40
   transposition on 43
Leedy, Douglas 7
Limit of frequency discrimination 13
Lute 71

M

Major-ninth chord 48
Major-seventh chord 48
Major scale
   five-limit
      constructing 39–40
Maxwell, Miles 54
McClain, Ernest G. 2
Mersenne, Marin 4
Microtones. *See also* Just Intervals
   eleven- and thirteen-limit 62
   seven-limit 54
Middle Ages 38
MIDI 76–79
   keyboard controller 78
   pitch bend 76–77
   using with tuning tables 78
   Tuning-Dump Specification 78–79
Minor-major-seventh chord 65
Minor-ninth chord 48
Minor-seventh chord 48

Minor-sixth chord 64
Missing fundamental. *See* Periodicity pitch

N

Neutral intervals 62
Nondominant-ninth chords 47
Nondominant-seventh chords 47
Notation for Just Intonation 32–33
   Ben Johnston's 33, 62
     Table 32
Novatone 71

O

Oboe 74
Odington, Walter 3
Oldani, Norbert 7
Oliveros, Pauline 70
1/1 (Journal of the Just Intonation Network) 8
One (foundation of all just tunings) 36
On the Sensations of Tone (book) 45
Orchestra 6
Other Music 7
Otonalities 29, 47. *See also* Harmonic series
Overtones. *See* Harmonics; Harmonic series; Partials

P

Partch, Harry 2, 6, 47, 58, 61, 62, 66, 67, 70, 71, 72
   tonality diamond 64
Partials 15. *See also* Harmonics; Harmonic series
   harmonic 15, 19–20
   inharmonic 15, 19
     of a free rectangular bar 72
     of a hinged bar 68
     of piano strings 67–69
Periodicity pitch 17–19, 20
   of eleven- and thirteen-limit dyads 61
   of just major triad 46
   of just minor triad 46–47
   of subharmonic pentad 58
   of subminor triad 57
Periodic vibration 9–10, 15
   amplitude 10
   frequency 10
   graph of 9
   period (τ) 10, 16
Phase Relationship 12
Piano 6, 35, 67–70
   single-strung 68
   tuning strategies 69
Pipe organ 70
Pitch 10. *See also* Periodic vibration: frequency
Pitch (periodical) 74
Place theory 18
Polansky, Larry 7
Primary interval
   defined 30
   for eleven (11:8) 61
   for five (5:4) 38
   for ninteen (19:16) 64
   for seventeen (17:16) 64
   for seven (7:4) 51
   for thirteen (13:8) 61
   for three (3:2) 36
   for two (2:1) 36
Prime limit 27, 35
   defined 30
Prime numbers 35
   defined 30
Psaltery 70, 72
Ptolemy, Claudius 2, 3, 39
Ptolemy's syntonon diatonic 33, 59. *See also* Major scale: five-limit
   complementation (figure) 44
   relative minor of 41
   tuning method (figure) 39
Pure tones 10, 15
   superposition of 11–12
Pythagoras of Samos 2, 36
Pythagorean comma 37–38, 44
Pythagorean diatonic scale 36–37, 40
Pythagorean tuning 2–3, 4, 36–38. *See also* Just Intonation, three-limit
   tendency of string players for 75

Q

Quartertone scale. *See* Temperament: twenty-four-tone equal

R

Rameau, Jean Philippe 4
Ratios. *See* Frequency ratios; Just Intervals
Ratios of eleven
   table 61
Ratios of thirteen
   table 62
Recorder 74
Reed instruments 19
Reed organ 70
Renaissance 3
Residue tone. *See* Periodicity pitch
Resultant tones. *See* Difference tones, Summation tones
Rich, Robert 7, 78
Riley, Terry 7, 69, 70, 75
   In C 7
Root (of a chord) 31
Rosenthal, David 72
Roughness 13, 20. *See also* Interference Beats

S

Sackbut 76
Sawtooth wave 16
Saxophone 74
Schmidt, Daniel 7, 72
Scholz, Carter 7, 78
Senario 3, 4
Septimal comma (64:63) 54, 65
Seven
   consonance of 35
7♭5 chord 64
7♯5 chord 65
Siegel, Jules 77

Simple harmonic motion 9. *See also* Sine wave
Simple tone 10
Sine wave 9, 10
Singing. *See* Voice
Special relationships 22–24
   absence of among eleven- and thirteen-limit dyads 59
   beyond the octave 23–24
   defined 22
   involving higher harmonics 24
   table 23
Sruti box 76
Stone, Tom 71
String players
   "natural tendencies" of 74
   use of vibrato 75
Subharmonic series 28–30
Subjective pitch. *See* Periodicity pitch
Subminor-seventh chord 58
Summation tones 16, 17
   first-order 17
Supermajor-seventh chord 59
Supertonic problem 40–42
Synthesizers. *See also* MIDI
   with user-programmable tuning tables 7, 77–78
   Yamaha DX/TX 77, 79
Syntonic comma 39, 41, 42, 44, 71
Syntonon diatonic. *See* Ptolemy's syntonon diatonic

T

Tamboura 76
Temperament
   defined 3
   meantone 3, 35, 42
   twelve-tone equal 4, 11, 33, 35, 37, 42, 49
     benefits 5
     deviation of harmonic series from 15
   twenty-four-tone equal 62
   well temperament 4, 35
Tempered major third 17, 23
Tenney, James 7
Tetrachordal genera 34, 59
Tetrachordal scales
   equal 34, 37, 40
   mixed 34
   seven-limit 59
     (figure) 60
Tetrachords 33–34, 55
   defined 33
   disjunct 34
   permutations 34
Tetrad. *See also* Dominant-seventh chord, Major-seventh chord, Minor-seventh chord
   subharmonic 58
Thompson, General Perronet 5, 71
Tied frets 71
Timbre 10, 19
Timing theory 18
Tone clusters 63
   eleven- and thirteen-limit 63
   seven-limit 56

Transposition 11
Triads
   augmented 48, 49–50, 65
   condissonant 47–48
   diminished 31, 35, 48, 51, 55, 56
      subharmonic 58
   dominant 39
   5:7:9 57
   4:6:7 57
      subharmonic 58
   major 31, 39, 46
      voicings in C (table) 30
   minor 31, 39, 41, 46
      proposed tuning with 19:16 64–65
      supertonic 41, 42
   open 38
   Pythagorean 38
      major 46
      minor 46
   subdominant 39
   subminor 31, 55, 57
   supermajor 58
   tonic 39
Trombone 76

Tuning
   History 2–7
Tuning and Temperament (book) 2
Twelfth root of two 11

U

Utonalities 29, 47, 58. *See also* Subharmonic series

V

Viol 71
Virtual pitch. *See* Periodicity pitch
Vogt, Walter 71
Voice 76

W

The Well-Tempered Clavier 4
Widener, Ward 64, 65
Wilson, Ervin
   combination product sets 64
Wind instruments 73–74
Wold, Erling 7

Y

Young, La Monte 7, 61, 69
   Dream Chords 38, 64, 65
   The Dream House 7
   5 V 67 6:38 PM NYC 65
   The Four Dreams of China 64, 76
   The Lower Map of The Eleven's Division in The Romantic Symmetry (over a 60 cycle base) in Prime Time from 122 to 119 with 144 65
   The Romantic Symmetry in Prime Time from 112 to 144 with 119 65
   The Second Dream of the High Tension Line Step-Down Transformer 64, 76
   The Subsequent Dreams of China 64
   The Theater of Eternal Music 7
   The Well-Tuned Piano 7, 65, 68

Z

Zarlino, Gioseffe 3
Zither 70

www.ingramcontent.com/pod-product-compliance
Lightning Source LLC
Chambersburg PA
CBHW061821290426
44110CB00027B/2937